'SOUTHERN ME[DLEY]

The R C 'Dick' Riley Archive Vol 3
Compiled by Mike King

The
· The Transport ·
Treasury

ISBN 978-1-913251-02-4

First Published in 2019 by Transport Treasury Publishing Ltd. 16 Highworth Close, High Wycombe, HP13 7PJ

www.ttpublishing.co.uk

Printed in the UK by Messrs. Henry Ling Ltd. Dorchester.

Contents

Front cover: Ex-LSWR T9 class 4-4-0 No. 30705 departs from Platform 10 at Waterloo on 7th September 1954, with the 1.54pm local service to Basingstoke – fast to Woking then calling at all stations. By this time, the T9s were becoming an unusual sight at Waterloo but remained on South Western section country area workings until 1961, particularly west of Exeter. *RCR 5475.*

Title page: Urie S15 class 4-6-0 No. 30513 resides inside Eastleigh running shed on 5th September 1954, shortly after receiving a general overhaul at the nearby works. Built in March 1921, the loco spent its entire life allocated to Strawberry Hill and its replacement steam shed, Feltham, until withdrawn in April 1963 with a final mileage of 1,231,659. Employed mainly on heavy goods trains to Southampton, Bournemouth and the West of England, these rugged 4-6-0s were the backbone of South Western section freights for many years – assisted by the Maunsell examples of the class after 1927. They could also be relied upon to haul relief passenger trains on Summer Saturdays. A Lord Nelson stands behind, while an O2 is on the left. Eastleigh shed was a large, 15-road building (plus a repair bay) with an allocation of over 120 locomotives in its heyday. It was one of the last to close to steam, on 9th July 1967 and, because of its proximity to the flightpath to Southampton Airport just next door, was soon demolished. A small diesel depot situated in the south-east corner has replaced it although the shed sidings remain for rolling stock stabling. *RCR 5463.*

Opposite: On 22nd May 1953, Bournemouth's West Country pacific No. 34044 *Woolacombe* awaits departure from platform 9 while Black 5 No. 45051 reverses on to its train in platform 8. The Stanier locomotive was one of the seven reallocated to Nine Elms while the Merchant Navy pacifics were out of action (see pages 28 & 29) for the emergency. A 4-COR electric stands in platform 7 with a Portsmouth service. "Blood and custard" (or crimson lake and cream, if you prefer the official description) coaches abound. *RCR4589.*

Rear cover: The interior of Walworth Coal Sidings Signal box on 1st March 1957. *RCR 10272.*

Introduction

Richard Calcott Riley was born in Lambeth on 2nd July 1921. Known to his friends as 'Dick', he took his first serious railway photographs in March 1937. Between then and 1967 he took almost 18,000 black and white pictures, with others in colour from 1953 onwards. Incidentally, for those wondering, the name Calcott was his mother's maiden name.

Growing up in South London, Dick soon developed an interest in the local railways and the LBSCR was one of his favourites – surpassed only by his love of the Great Western. It was in this context that I first made contact with him, sometime in the 1970s, with a query about Brighton brake vans. Once convinced of my serious interest, he responded generously and most helpfully and he continued to do so for me for the rest of his life. His sources of photographs (not just those of his own taking) enhanced the various Southern wagon books that I co-authored with Alan Blackburn, Gerry Bixley and Ray Chorley and, later, the various carriage stock books of my own all had contributions from Dick's collections. Many other authors were to find exactly the same response to their enquiries. He also gave me sound advice about keeping good accounts of my own publishing ventures – advice that I continue to use to this day. Clearly, Dick's lifetime in banking and finance were put to good use in this field.

As a boy, he attended Mercer's School near Holborn Viaduct. On leaving in 1938, he joined the City banking firm of Glyn Mills & Company. Wartime service with the Territorial Army and then the Royal Engineers followed, including a stint at Longmoor and a period in Normandy during 1944/45, before resuming his banking career with Glyn Mills. Living for much of his life at Tulse Hill, Dick was well placed to visit most areas of the Southern and here we have a selection of some 140 taken between 1950 and 1966 – all on the Southern Region. They are not necessarily arranged in chronological order but some have been placed into themed subject areas such as shed scenes, electric stock, steam-hauled rolling stock, Pullmans and the like. Others are simply interesting subjects in their own right.

Dick was fortunate to be acquainted with many of the leading railwaymen of the day, which allowed access to locations not always accessible to others. Sometimes, however, he managed unofficial footplate rides and in a letter to David Gould dated November 1982 he recounts a trip on the 4.55pm Tunbridge Wells West to East Grinstead train where he fired Q class 0-6-0 30541 – now preserved on the Bluebell Railway. The letter states that the crew made him work hard that afternoon but he thoroughly enjoyed the experience!! Unfortunately we do not know the exact date but it must have been pre-1955. He was always careful to record the names and addresses of the crews concerned – supplying them with copies of any pictures taken on the journeys. Dick was also an ardent supporter of the Bluebell Railway and was much involved with the line during its earlier days. Indeed, my last meeting with him was at Sheffield Park station one hot day not long before he died in July 2006. He was clearly in discomfort through arthritis but was determined to enjoy the day out.

It was around this time that he decided to pass all his black & white photographs to the Transport Treasury to ensure that they could be made available to all who were interested. We hope you enjoy this selection – there could easily be more at a later date!

Mike King. East Preston, July 2019.

Opposite: Cannon Street, 1954 viewed south along Platform 7 with a pair of 4-SUB electrics in the platform – the nearer an all-steel Bulleid unit, the farther an older wooden-bodied LSWR unit. The overall roof is now minus most of its glazing (hence the individual platform canopies) and removal would be started in 1958. Today, only the end piers plus sections of the flank walls remain whilst the towers are listed structures. The station has been much renovated in recent years and no longer looks anything like it does in these pictures – but maybe that isn't such a bad thing! (See also views of Cannon Street on page 30.) *RCR 5636.*

Stewarts Lane is chiefly remembered for providing the motive power for the prestigious *Golden Arrow* and *Night Ferry* services – and here we have two for the price of one – a scene not often captured by enthusiasts! On the left is West Country No. 34091 *Weymouth*, with the full *Golden Arrow* regalia – and spotlessly clean of course – while on the right is Merchant Navy No. 35028 *Clan Line*, complete with *Night Ferry* headboard. Not quite as clean but probably the BR power class 8 rating of the larger engine. The date is 15th June 1958. The two make an interesting comparison in front ends – not quite as similar as many would believe. No. 34091 dates from September 1949 and was the first of the final batch of light pacifics – the last to receive an official naming ceremony and the first to sport British Railways dark green livery. She went new to Stewarts Lane then and stayed until May 1961 and the completion of Phase 2 of the Kent Coast electrification, moving to Salisbury until withdrawal in 1964. She was one of few unrebuilt light pacifics to retain the original 9ft wide 5,500 gallon tender throughout, even when the side raves were cut down. No. 35028 was new in December 1948, being allocated to Bournemouth for a year before moving to Dover in October 1949 and to Stewarts Lane some six months later. Remaining on the Eastern section until withdrawn for rebuilding in August 1959, she was often in charge of boat trains as well as the two named expresses. After rebuilding, she moved to Nine Elms and Weymouth while since 1967 her exploits in preservation have been well recorded. It is sobering to think that *Clan Line* has now been in preservation for well over twice as long as BR ownership – although of course, not looking like she does here. *RCR 12031.*

Chapter 1
Works and Shed Scenes

We will start with a selection of these, beginning at Stewarts Lane. Some were almost certainly official society visits of some sort, others were entirely unofficial or, in quite a few instances, at the invitation of senior members of shed staff, often tipping Dick off to something interesting.

A general view of Stewarts Lane shed, taken from the former LCDR viaduct carrying trains passing to and from Victoria (Eastern section) station, looking roughly westwards, on 10th May 1959. The 16-road north light truss roof running shed, dating from 1934 may be seen; with the far right pair of gables under repair – this section having been walled off and being made ready to service diesel locomotives. A good selection of steam locomotives may be seen outside, including (from left to right) a C class 0-6-0, LMR Fairburn 2-6-4 tank,U1 class mogul No. 31906, two E2 class 0-6-0 tanks flanking H class tank No. 31265 and a BR standard 5. Beyond the shed, in the haze a SECR D1/E1 4-4-0 keeps company with a 350hp diesel shunter (the only obvious bit of modernity visible), with another mogul behind. To the right is the coaling plant, with a line of loco coal wagons, another C class goods and a Bulleid pacific. In fact, one other aspect of modernisation may be seen – the DC third rails alongside the tracks in the foreground. Phase 1 of the Kent Coast electrification would be inaugurated within a month and the depot's steam allocation would start to decline. It had been the largest shed on the Southern Railway with over 150 locomotives allocated – but this was about to change. In former LCDR/SECR days the location was better known as Longhedge, later Battersea and the name Stewarts Lane was only applied from the 1930s onwards. In the background the ex-LBSCR South London line viaduct crosses the site – just seen above the shed roof. For the enthusiast the shed was a particularly difficult one to "bunk" as public access points were few and well-guarded and the best views were often to be had only from trains crossing the viaducts. Dick Riley was a regular visitor to the shed – perhaps because of his friendship with one-time shedmaster Dick Hardy. Living in Tulse Hill, it was also probably his local shed! *RCR 13280.*

Above: Between 1952 and 1958, perhaps for reasons of publicity and prestige more than practicality, Stewarts Lane had two Britannia pacifics allocated and these were regular performers on the *Golden Arrow* and other boat trains, but seemingly not on the *Night Ferry*. The two were No. 70004 *William Shakespeare* and No. 70014 *Iron Duke* and here the latter is ready to back down to Victoria for the 1pm working to Folkestone Junction on 27th February 1957, Stewarts Lane duty 4. After turning at the small shed there, the loco would then haul the empty stock, tender first, to Dover Marine, before going on shed

at Dover to be serviced before the return working at just before 6pm. It was not exactly an onerous life and the two Brits were returned to the LM Region in mid-1958, to be replaced by BR standard 5 engines Nos. 73041/42 – nothing like as glamorous but maybe more useful! This view is looking towards Victoria with the ex-LCDR viaduct in the background – from where Dick took the first picture in this selection of Stewarts Lane shed. The shed building is behind us. Note the ex-LSWR 700 class goods on the extreme left – probably on a trip goods or milk train working from Clapham yard. We can also guess the consequences of failing to heed the instruction on the noticeboard! *RCR 12019.*

This page: Staying with Stewarts Lane, on 10th May 1959 original Bulleid Merchant Navy pacific No. 35001 *Channel Packet* stands outside the shed carrying the dark blue *Night Ferry* headboard with the familiar back scene of Hampton's depository behind. The air-smoothed casing is already on at least its third incarnation, while the tender has been cut down and makes a poor match for the locomotive. Not that the casing is now very smooth as there are many dents, ripples and repairs evident. Indeed, the locomotive would within days be withdrawn for rebuilding – one of the last three of the class to be dealt with – and this would take place at Eastleigh Works between 27th May and August 1959. Despite imminent rebuilding, she is still rostered for the Night Ferry – a train that could, on occasion, reach 19 vehicles and be as heavy as 825 tons – although the usual load was somewhat less on most nights. This was *Channel Packet's* second period of service on the Eastern section. The first was briefly in April 1946, appropriately for the inaugural post-war *Golden Arrow*, the second from January 1957 until May 1959. Along with Nos. 35001/28, rebuilt Merchant Navy No. 35015 *Rotterdam Lloyd* was also at Stewarts Lane between 1956 and 1959 and could also be seen hauling boat trains and the *Golden Arrow* together with the two original examples. One cannot help but think that Dick had been advised of *Channel Packet's* impending rebuild and made a special journey to "The Lane" to record the event. *RCR 13272.*

A final view of 35028 reversing out of the shed yard prior to picking up empty stock for Victoria which will be taken tender-first into the terminus. The loco will then probably work a later boat train to either Folkestone or Dover. Note the three clips on the body sheeting above the nameplate – used to mount the large "golden arrow". The date is 16th August 1959 and by this time *Clan Line* was the only original Merchant Navy remaining on the Eastern section (No. 35006 was similarly still active on the South Western section) and would be called into Eastleigh Works for rebuilding just five days later. Was Dick tipped off about this – almost certainly!! The loco is about to pass beneath the ex-LCDR lines into Victoria while behind may be seen the rather brutal architecture of Stewarts Lane signal box – a wartime replacement for the previous pre-Grouping style cabin, destroyed by a flying bomb on 31st July 1944. The replacement was needed in a hurry and so practicality rather than aesthetics won the day. The original lever frame got reused which must have speeded the rebuilding process somewhat. The adjacent footbridge was one of the few access points into the shed for pedestrians. *RCR 14136.*

The more mundane at Stewarts Lane. C class 0-6-0 No. 31037 stands at the head of a line of engines between the coaling plant and the turntable on 16th August 1959. The South London line viaduct may be seen behind with the Battersea Park colour light home signal thereon. The C's were one of the first designs to appear after the amalgamation of the SER and LCDR in 1899 and some would claim that they were almost pure LCDR Robert Surtees in origin – LCDR class B3 rather than SECR C! Whatever the case, they proved an excellent investment and a total of 109 were completed over the period 1900-8 by Ashford, Longhedge, Neilson Reid and Sharp Stewart & Co. No. 31037 dates from March 1901 and lasted until February 1961 and was one of those constructed at Ashford Works. She carries a 74A (Ashford) shedplate, but would end her days working from Guildford – one of a handful to be transferred there. Apart from No. 1685 which was rebuilt as the unique S class saddle tank shunter in 1917, all the other 108 examples lasted until 1947, with the last two remaining in departmental service at Ashford Wagon Works until as late as 1966/67, from where No. 31592 was purchased by the Bluebell Railway and may be enjoyed operating on the line to this day. Behind is W class 2-6-4 tank No. 31921 – a Hither Green resident in 1958. *RCR 14133.*

This page: Another class much associated with Stewarts Lane were the H class tanks. On 15th June 1958 No. 31552 is posed with crew, shed staff and visitors – passed fireman Charlie Watson, Richard Hardy and son James on the footplate while Fred Pankhurst and grandson, fitter Alf Prater and an unknown fireman stand in front. There were 66 of these handsome locomotives and those at "The Lane" could be seen on empty stock workings into and out of Victoria until June 1961. No. 31552 dates from January 1905 and would last until November 1961 – one of few not to receive SR air-controlled pull-push gear between 1949 and 1960. Note the worksplate on the splasher – proudly proclaiming the SE&CR and Ashford Works – where all 66 members of the class were built. All except two were completed in the years 1904-9 but when Richard Maunsell replaced Harry Wainwright in charge at Ashford in December 1913 questions were then asked as to what had become of the final pair. It transpired that all materials except the boilers were to hand but construction had not been undertaken – symptomatic of the lax management situation that brought about Wainwright's enforced resignation, perhaps? Maunsell soon had this matter remedied and the final two (SECR Nos. 16 and 184) duly appeared in 1915. *RCR 12035.*

Opposite: Stewarts Lane also played host to various foreign locomotives off cross-London freight trains. Here, on 23rd August 1958 ex-LBSCR E6 radial tank No. 32413 from Norwood Junction keeps company with an unidentified LNER J50 0-6-0 tank, parked in a siding alongside the tracks leading from Stewarts Lane towards Clapham Junction and the West London line. The J50 has probably come in from Hornsey via Kensington Olympia. The E6 was built at Brighton in July 1905 and for a short period carried the name *Fenchurch*, the second LBSCR engine to do so, running until November 1958 – one of a class of just 12 engines. Behind the locomotives may be seen an elderly timber-framed 5-plank open wagon and a LSWR Diagram 1410 sliding-door goods van – probably in departmental use for locomotive stores or the like. The unusually quiet (for a Saturday afternoon) coaling plant may be seen on the right. Note also the timber trestles used to access locomotive footplates beside these tracks. *RCR 12632.*

The new order at Stewarts Lane. What we later knew as class 71 electric locomotive No. E5010 (later No. 71010) is parked in the fork of the shed entrance on 7th November 1959. A total of 24 of these 2,552hp machines were built at Doncaster between 1958 and 1960, primarily for the few remaining loco-hauled trains such as the *Golden Arrow* and *Night Ferry*, plus express freight services between the Channel ports and London. They were equipped to run both on the 750 volt DC network and also using overhead power via the centrally-mounted pantograph on the roof – however few locations were so provided and the pantographs saw relatively little use. They were remarkably powerful for their size and could competently handle the fully loaded *Night Ferry* unaided, easily reaching their design maximum speed of 90mph. Finished in bright malachite green with white cab window surrounds and a white/red/white horizontal stripe along the sides, they also looked very smart when new, although E5010 appears to have already lost its initial shine. Ten locomotives were modified in 1967/68 as class 74 electro-diesels, however accommodating the additional diesel generating equipment within the existing bodywork proved difficult and the rebuilds were not entirely successful. As a result, these were withdrawn relatively soon after, while the demise of loco-hauled trains and freight services saw the remaining original class 71 locomotives withdrawn by 1977. No. E5001 is preserved in the National Collection and is currently on show at NRM Shildon. *RCR 14418*.

Motor luggage van (MLV) S68001 is seen when new in approximately the same location on 14th June 1959. An original prototype MLV (E68000) was built at Eastleigh for the South Tyneside electric system in 1955, for parcels traffic and two similar vehicles (S68001/2) were completed in 1959 for Phase 1 of the Kent Coast electrification. These were followed by eight more (S68003-10) in 1961 for Phase 2 which differed in some minor details from the original pair. They were intended for Continental boat train service, providing additional luggage accommodation and would usually run at the London end of a rake of 4-CEP/BEP/CEP vehicles between Victoria and Folkestone/Dover but they could also run independently on occasions – sometimes hauling a tail load of one or two vans – for which purpose they were originally both Westinghouse and vacuum-braked. They were also equipped with batteries to enable them to run over short distances of non-electrified tracks at Folkestone and Dover – albeit at slow speed only. Some boat trains later required the use of two vans leading to 14-coach formations being seen, but later six standard BR full brakes were electrically wired to remove the need for this duplication and these were described as TLV's (trailer luggage vans). The later BR classification for the MLV's was class 419. The need for motor luggage vans on boat trains declined as the 1980s progressed and ended completely with the opening of the Channel Tunnel. The vans were then used on a variety of parcels services around the Southern Region being finally transferred to departmental use by 1991. Since withdrawal most have passed into preservation. Interestingly, they have carried a variety of different liveries during their lives, including Southern Region green, BR corporate blue or blue and grey, Network South East "jaffa-cake" and "toothpaste stripe" colours while two received the colourful Royal Mail red livery in 1988. Regrettably, after a robbery this distinctive pair were then reliveried in "toothpaste stripe" to reduce the conspicuous colours. In the picture, work to electrify many of the depot roads is progressing, while behind the motor luggage van is a Southern 15-ton ballast dropside wagon (Diagram 1773) loaded with a compressor to provide power for the construction work. *RCR 13653*.

A Bulleid – but not as most of us would know it! Ill-fated "Leader" class locomotives 36002/3 (the latter in skeletal form nearest) in store at Bognor shed on 1ˢᵗ July 1950. At this time prototype locomotive No. 36001 was undergoing main line trials between Eastleigh and Woking – the only one of the class to ever run in steam. However, No. 36002 (seen inside the shed) was only days away from completion before the trials were halted and the whole scheme abandoned. By this time, Bulleid had left BR for Ireland and soon after the press had got hold of the story – blowing things out of all proportion – and the two uncompleted locomotives were deliberately moved to an out-of-the-way location and away from public gaze. For a fuller account, readers should consult the books by Kevin Robertson from Alan Sutton Publishing dated 1988 and 1990, and the revised and rewritten account published by Ian Allan; 2008. The trials were not very successful – mostly for technical reasons (remember post-war austerity Britain was an impoverished country) – but others claim that they were deliberately sabotaged by staff and trade unions owing to the intolerable working conditions on the footplate of the locomotive. Certainly, some of the trials were completed using volunteer rather than "press-ganged" staff who got involved for the interest rather than just as part of the job. Whatever the truth, Bulleid's challenge to traditional steam locomotive construction failed and we will never know if such a revolutionary design might have been successful had the railway persevered a little longer. Bognor shed saw relatively little steam after the mid-Sussex line electrification in 1938 – mostly the daily goods train and weekend excursions to the seaside town so it was a good place to store surplus locomotives. Also seen on the left is Hall & Company's coal yard, while the tender of a Brighton loco, possibly a C2X goods, is visible through the shed building. *RCR 4051.*

Above: Superannuated but not quite redundant. Former SER O class 0-6-0 No. A98 at Ramsgate shed on 6th April 1953, engaged as a stationary boiler supplying steam for carriage heating purposes. Dating from September 1899, she ran until October 1929 before being "grounded" at Ramsgate. One of no less than 122 engines built between 1878 and 1899, they became the standard South Eastern Railway heavy goods engines, being seen anywhere on the system between Ramsgate and Reading. Rebuilding to class O1 began in 1903 and 59 of the class were so modified, extending their lives to, in a few instances, 1961. A total of 31 unmodified examples came to the Southern Railway in 1923 but withdrawal of these commenced immediately, to be completed by February 1932. No. A98 (it never received its allocated post-1931 number, which would have been 1098) remained on this duty at Ramsgate until later in 1953, when it was replaced by D class 4-4-0 No. 31501. The curious-looking wagon behind the locomotive is one of the four SR snowploughs numbered S1-S4 – a design "cribbed" from the North Eastern Railway who had several similar vehicles and no doubt had greater need of them "oop north" than did the Southern. That said however, heavy snowfalls were by no means unknown in Kent. In the left background, locomotives visible include Q1 class no. 33022 and a D1/E1 4-4-0. (The top of the chimney is cut-off on the negative.) *RCR 4458.*

Right: Although not a shed as such, there were a number of locations where turning, coaling and servicing facilities were available. One of these was at Brockenhurst – adjacent to the marshalling yard on the down side of the line. T9 No. 30729 takes water from the simple LSWR-style water column adjacent to the turntable on 8th September 1953. The turntable was regularly used on Summer Saturdays to turn the locomotives hauling the Lymington Pier through services, as facilities down the branch were restricted and very often a smaller locomotive (such as a Q class 0-6-0) would be needed to take the train onward and return it to the main line

later in the day. The turntable itself was 49ft 11in diameter, so could not accommodate anything larger than a 4-4-0, ensuring that such through trains were not entrusted to anything longer. The last steam locomotives employed were the Schools class, after which Crompton diesels took over before through trains ceased in about 1966. Note that the turntable entry is "guarded" by a Westinghouse disc shunt signal and this is "off", indicating that the T9 will shortly move onto the 'table to turn. No. 30729 would last until March 1961, running latterly over the North Cornwall line to Padstow or to Plymouth. In the sidings behind, a rake of GWR coaches may be seen, while above these the footbridge crossing the western end of the station platforms is just visible. *RCR 4792.*

Opposite: A view at Basingstoke shed, taken on 12th September 1954. This shows, amongst other things, the coaling plant situated just to the west of the 3-road shed building. What brought Dick to Basingstoke on that day was the running of *"The Farnborough Flyer"* – a special train from Leeds and back hauled by preserved GNR Atlantic No. 251 and GCR D11 class Director No. 62663 *Prince Albert*, seen here having turned and being coaled ready for the return journey. Passengers then went on to Farnborough air show by SR train services and back to Basingstoke in time for the return of the special to Leeds in the early evening. Also visible is an SR N15X 4-6-0 coupled to the LNER beaver-tail observation car, which also needed to be turned before recoupling to the rear of the special train. On the right is a selection of loco coal wagons – both ancient and modern. The former are represented by RCH standard 7-plank 13-ton wooden bodied vehicles, the latter by BR 16-ton all-steel mineral wagons. One of the wooden wagons just shows faded private-owner lettering "ICI". The up yard and the main line towards Worting Junction may be seen in the distance, while a Maunsell open saloon third coach stands at the buffer stops in the left foreground – perhaps having run a hot axle box earlier and needing to be detached from an up express. It was certainly not the ideal location to park a passenger coach – near to all that coal dust! *RCR 5498.*

Above: Taken on the same day we see Urie N15 class 4-6-0 No. 30745 *Tintagel,* resplendent in BR dark green livery carried since August 1951. The twenty original engines in the class were built as unnamed 4-6-0s by the LSWR in 1918-23 and their initial performance was slightly disappointing. After the Grouping, Maunsell realised that with a little modification this could be much improved while the Southern's newly appointed Public Relations Officer, John Elliot, saw merit in naming the locomotives after characters and places of Arthurian legend. This gave rise, so the story goes, to Maunsell's dry comment "It doesn't matter what you call them, it won't make them go any faster!" However, as a publicity idea, it was a stroke of genius and the class became firm favourites of enthusiasts and the travelling public alike. No. 30745 received Southern Railway livery in September 1924, was named in April 1925 and continued to run until February 1956, having been based at Basingstoke since 1950. In this view we may see the cab interior and the coal load – which does not all look of good quality. Behind is Eli Lilly & Company's sports field – their modernistic UK head office (built in 1938) and manufacturing base is out of sight to the right of the picture but is visible in the view opposite. Their private siding, coal dock and boiler house may be seen immediately behind 30745's tender. Eli Lilley are an American firm who specialise in pharmaceutical and biological products and are still in business today. Not so for No. 30745 or Basingstoke shed although the name was later carried by BR standard 5 No. 73084. *RCR 5497.*

Staying with the theme of ex-LSWR 4-6-0s here are H15 class engines Nos. 30335 and 30334 in store at Salisbury on 14th May 1955. Both have sacking over their chimneys but would return to traffic in time for the summer service and each have a few years life left in them yet. The 26 locomotives constituting the H15 class were something of a mixed bunch. Nos. 482-491 were the original Urie engines of 1914, while Nos. 473-478 and 521-524 were of Maunsell design and date from 1924. No. 335 was Urie's rebuild of the solitary Drummond E14 class 4-6-0, completed in 1914 – this engine easily being the worst of all the Drummond 4-6-0 classes while Nos. 330-334 were Maunsell rebuilds of Drummond's F13 engines – not quite as bad as the E14 but still not worth keeping in their original form. The six Drummond rebuilds were always difficult engines to fire so they were concentrated at Salisbury shed for most of their lives, where the crews got used to their foibles and were able to make the best of them. Occasionally one was loaned to Nine Elms or Feltham but soon returned to Salisbury, probably with a note saying "thanks, but no thanks" – or words to that effect! Once all the King Arthurs were in service, the Salisbury H15's were relegated to local passenger turns to Exeter or Waterloo or heavy freight duties but could often be stored at off-peak times – as seen here. Despite this, all except one put in more than a million miles in traffic. The various differences between the two locomotives (and their tenders) may be appreciated, while next door is snowplough S2 – hopefully not needed until the next winter. In the background, the usual Salisbury allocation of moguls, an M7 and a Bulleid pacific may be seen. *RCR 5741.*

At the rear of Ryde St Johns loco shed is ex-LBSCR E1 class 0-6-0T No. W1 Medina, in the process of being cut up, seen on 25th June 1957. Following improvements made at Medina Wharf in 1932 – the main entry point for coal on the Isle of Wight – four E1 class locomotives were transferred to the Island in order to haul the 40-wagon coal trains that could now be dealt with at the new facility. No W1 was previously SR No. B136 (ex-LBSCR *Brindisi* of 1879). Most of the coal was destined for household use, while some went for gas production, and the rest was hauled to Newport or Ryde for locomotive purposes. Inevitably, in the 1950s demand declined and although the E1 class locomotives were used on passenger work, the need for all four gradually fell away. No. W2 Yarmouth was the first to be withdrawn (in September 1956) but No. W1 followed six months later, leaving No. W3 Ryde and No. W4 Wroxall to soldier on until 1959/60 respectively – presumably as they became due for shopping. In true Island fashion, anything that could be reused was stripped from the locomotive, but with the impending withdrawal of the other E1s, use of the major parts was somewhat limited. As far as the Isle of Wight was concerned – that would be the end of the E1 story – but not if the present-day Isle of Wight Steam Railway has anything to do with it! One more E1 loco has survived – No. B110 – which was sold to the Cannock & Rugeley Colliery Company as long ago as April 1927, where it was named Cannock Wood and allocated the running number 9.It passed to the West Midlands Railway Preservation Society in 1963 but little restoration was possible until the locomotive was moved to the East Somerset Railway at Cranmore in 1978. It ran there during the 1990s but in 2011 was moved to Haven Street for eventual restoration as W2 Yarmouth. Currently it may be seen there, cosmetically restored to BR unlined black livery. Once operational again, the arrangement is that it will divide its time between the Isle of Wight Railway and the East Somerset Railway. Behind the partially dismantled loco, one of the LBSCR 5-plank 10-ton open goods wagons may be see – some 455 of these were transferred to the Island from 1925 onwards but by 1957 only about 150 remained. This is No. S27887 which was renumbered and shipped over in 1947 – the very last one. *RCR 10836.*

Opposite page, top: Original Merchant Navy No. 35005 *Canadian Pacific* displays its massive bulk at Nine Elms on 6th September 1958. This was one of the second batch of the class, completed between September 1941 and July 1942 – characterised by the asbestos-based "limpet board" casing

with strengthening rib just above the nameplate. She entered service on 13th January 1942, allocated to Salisbury shed, but tended to shuttle between Exmouth Junction and Nine Elms over the period late 1942 to 1959, when withdrawn for rebuilding, after which she operated from Bournemouth and Weymouth sheds. From March 1948 until March 1951 the locomotive was fitted with a mechanical stoker with a view to seeing whether this might make firing easier and so improve performance. The general consensus was that it did not and no other member of the class was so equipped – perhaps to the disappointment of firemen! The air-smoothed casing style seen here dates from April 1944 – the front end cowl was fitted then, although the fairing ahead of the cylinders has already been removed. The tender (not the one paired with originally) is still in original form and would not be cut down until the locomotive was rebuilt. After withdrawal on 10th October 1965, the loco was stored at Feltham and then Weymouth before being sold to Woodham Brothers; remaining in Barry scrapyard from April 1966 until March 1973 when sold into preservation. After several moves, the loco returned to main line service between 1998 and 2002, painted in the short-lived BR express blue livery which was carried by the loco in original condition from February 1950 until February 1954. It then ran (in green livery) on the Mid-Hants Railway until 2008 and is now at Eastleigh Works undergoing a major overhaul – and expected to return to steam in 2021. *RCR 12724.*

Opposite page, bottom: A view of the "country" end of the former LCDR Gillingham shed, taken on 30th September 1958. Trackwork alterations are in progress ready for the extension of the electrification to Margate and Ramsgate, which would be fully operational from June 1959, although the shed itself closed in June 1960. Known originally as New Brompton when first opened, the station was from 1939 until 1959 the terminating point for outer suburban electrified services from London. Once full electrification extended eastwards, the shed lost its permanent allocation for the final year and was later demolished; the site now occupied by industrial development. The allocation comprised up to 50 locomotives: 0-4-4 tanks, 0-6-0 and 4-4-0 tender locomotives predominated. Visible is L1 class No. 31786, built by the North British Locomotive Company in April 1926 and allocated to Gillingham from May 1955 until transferred to Nine Elms in June 1959. The locomotive was destined to be the last of the class in service and was finally withdrawn in February 1962 – having spent its final months on empty stock and van trains in the south west London area. Also visible is the brake end of a SECR "birdcage" coach – probably part of the breakdown crane set – and there is a C class 0-6-0 shunting in the yard beyond. The line on the far right, disappearing beneath the brick bridge is the branch to Chatham Dockyard, describing a somewhat circular route into the dockyard, entering then from a northerly direction. The connecting line remains in place but was truncated some distance from the docks after they closed to naval activity in March 1984 and has seen no traffic for some years past. *RCR 12804.*

Above: The Gillingham crane DS202 and its match truck DS3089 on 23rd May 1959, together with the end of a SECR "birdcage" coach – quite possibly the one seen in the previous picture. Both vehicles have interesting histories. The crane dates from 1899 and was built for the SER by Cowans Sheldon of Carlisle, becoming crane No. L3 at Ashford shed. It later moved to Stewarts Lane and then Gillingham and was withdrawn in November 1962. It was of 15 tons capacity. The match truck was not the original match truck converted to run with the crane (that was a former SER 2-plank ballast wagon) but was rebuilt in March 1932 from a former Somerset & Dorset Joint Railway 2-plank open wagon dating from 1912; S&DJR No. 158, later LSWR No. 15059 and then SR No. 423 to Diagram 1307. It was then renumbered 202sm (to go with the crane, which by then carried the SR number 202s). For its new role it received extended side planking and the timber trestle – to support the crane jib. Renumbered yet again to DS3089 in January 1951, it was finally withdrawn in February 1962. By then almost certainly the last surviving ex-S&DJR wagon on the Southern Region – if not on BR, and equally remarkable in carrying no less than five numbers in its 60 year life! *RCR 13367.*

At Brighton shed on 23rd June 1956 is ex-LBSCR H2 class Atlantic No. 32421 *South Foreland*. This was one of eleven 4-4-2 tender locomotives built for the LBSCR between 1905 and 1912 – of two classes: H1 and H2 – the latter a superheated version of the former. The design originated with H. A. Ivatt of the Great Northern Railway, whose assistant, Douglas Earle Marsh became Locomotive, Carriage & Wagon Superintendent at Brighton Works in 1905, following the death of Robert Billinton. There was an urgent need for more powerful locomotives, so Marsh turned to his former boss's design and ordered five rather similar locomotives from Kitson & Company – becoming class H1 on the LBSCR and delivered in late 1905/ early 1906. They proved successful in service and after Marsh was forced to retire in 1911 – ill health was the reason given – his successor Lawson Billinton (son of Robert Billinton) repeated the process by building six more Atlantics at Brighton Works to form class H2. All eleven locomotives served the LBSCR and the Southern until withdrawals started in 1944. The Southern publicity department wished all SR passenger locomotives to carry names, so these were christened after well-known South Coast and West Country landmarks. The H2's – being the younger class – lasted longer and five of the six were still running in 1956 when a seemingly unrelated incident on the Eastern Region caused a problem.

On 1st September 1955 the unique LNER W1 4-6-4 No. 60700 was derailed at Westwood Junction near Peterborough. The cause was investigated and found to be a fracture of the bogie frame. Any locomotive with similar bogies were then examined and this included the H2 Atlantics. Two, including No. 32421 were found to be suspect and were taken out of service soon after, while two more only lasted a few months longer. So, when photographed at Brighton in March 1956, *South Foreland* had only a matter of weeks remaining in traffic before withdrawal. No. 32424 *Beachy Head* fared somewhat better and lasted until April 1958. Readers may be aware that the Bluebell Railway is constructing a replica of *Beachy Head* at Sheffield Park and this is expected to enter service in 2021. When that day comes there will be many "Brighton" enthusiasts who will be very pleased indeed. Dick too would surely have approved. *RCR 7380.*

Maunsell U class mogul No. 31794 stands on No. 2 road inside Yeovil Town shed on 10th July 1956. The shed at this location was built by the Salisbury and Yeovil Railway (soon to become part of the LSWR) in 1861 – a substantial 3-road brick structure – which survived until the end of steam working in the area. It closed officially on 12th June 1965 but continued to stable diesel units until 5th May 1968, on which date the Yeovil Junction to Pen Mill shuttle service ceased. The site was used for a further couple of years as a reception centre for recovered track and railway equipment before the shed was demolished and the area turned into the inevitable car park. The mogul is one of six (Nos. 31790-95) rebuilt "River" class tanks allocated to Yeovil from 1932 until at least 1958 where they were much used on local passenger trains between Salisbury and Exeter. Visible to the left is one of the pair of M7 0-4-4 tanks used on the Yeovil Town-Junction pull-push shuttle while the depot coaling crane may just be seen on the right. *RCR 7555.*

Another 3-road brick-built shed, but at a very different location and with a very different history. Ex-SER R1 class 0-6-0 tank No. 31174 and prospective replacement GWR pannier tank No. 9770 share the interior of Folkestone Junction shed with a Wickham permanent way trolley on 25th October 1958. The shed opened in 1900, replacing a single road structure on the other side of the line and served mainly to stable the harbour branch locomotives and to service those main line locomotives working the boat trains. Its allocation for many years included half a dozen R/R1 class tanks, but would not do so for very much longer. Ex-GWR tank No. 9770 arrived for trials at the beginning of October 1958 which proved successful and from March 1959 six others (Nos. 4601/10/16/26/30/31) arrived to take over from the ex-SER engines. Once given some attention at Ashford Works, the newcomers were found to be more powerful and could manage to lift the heavy boat trains up from the harbour with three engines per train (two at the front and one at the rear) whereas the R1s needed four on the same duties. This all came to an end in June 1961 with the inauguration of Phase 2 of the Kent Coast electrification and the shed closed soon after. Your writer came to know Folkestone Junction in the late 1950s and it was a wonderful place from which to watch the trains – and could recount a few interesting anecdotes - but doubtless the general public held a rather less enthusiastic view! *RCR 12920.*

An interesting comparison outside Eastleigh Works on 25th August 1957. On the left is N15X 4-6-0 No. 32331 – now relieved of its *Beattie* nameplates – standing alongside BR Class 4 mogul No. 76027 from Bournemouth (71B) shed. The former was withdrawn from service just a month earlier – the last of the class in traffic, while the BR mogul was in for a general overhaul. The seven locomotives of class N15X were rebuilds of the Brighton L class Baltic tanks, made redundant on electrification of the lines to Eastbourne and Hastings in 1935. Between December 1934 and April 1936 all were rebuilt and sent to Nine Elms, where they were put to work on the same rosters as the King Arthur's and Lord Nelson's. However, they were soon found wanting on such onerous duties and before long were relegated to semi-fasts, excursions and other more seasonal trains. However, at Nine Elms the fact that they were ex-Brighton engines might have also had something to do with their poor performance! Nevertheless, Bulleid made some minor alterations to the class which enabled them to continue in revenue-earning service until 1955-57, all working latterly from Basingstoke shed. The BR moguls were replacements for ex-LSWR 4-4-0s in the Eastleigh/Salisbury/Bournemouth area, dating from 1952 onwards and were extremely capable machines. A total of 37 were eventually allocated to the region and ten remained serviceable at the end of Southern steam on 9th July 1967. In the background behind No. 76027 is the preserved T3 4-4-0 No. 563 – now scheduled for overhaul and return to steam on the Swanage Railway. *RCR 11129.*

Chapter 2

Stations

Moving on to station scenes, we start at Clapham Junction. Situated in the fork of lines between the ex-LSWR routes to Reading and to Bournemouth/Weymouth etc. were 49 carriage sidings, which serviced almost all of the steam-hauled rolling stock used to and from Waterloo. In terms of train movements, it is Britain's busiest station and in steam days required a considerable number of pilot locomotives – both to shunt and remarshal trains but also to haul empty stock into and out of the terminus. Many classes of locomotive were employed – from LSWR, LBSCR and SECR, Southern and BR origins and there would always be something of interest to see. On 7th July 1950, ex-LBSCR E4 radial tank No. 32500 is engaged on shunting duties and is seen coupled to shunting truck S61323 – one of a pair regularly used to assist the shunting staff with their duties. Clapham yard was one of very few locations on the Southern where loose shunting of passenger stock was permitted and these trucks facilitated the process. They would also give the shunting staff something to ride upon; safer than clinging on to the side of carriages – not that it stopped this dangerous procedure – and gave them somewhere to store their shunting poles, sprags, spare coupling hooks etc. This particular example was built on a former LSWR tender chassis. The E4 dates from 1900 and was formerly LBSCR *Puttenham* – in fact a Surrey village in LSWR territory! At the time it was the only member of the class allocated to Nine Elms and would last until 1962 – by which time it had returned to the Central section. *RCR 4053.*

Moving up the line to Waterloo, we find something rather different. This and the next picture were taken on 20th and 21st May 1953 and show an unusual selection of locomotives. Going back a few weeks, on 24th April Merchant Navy pacific No. 35020 *Bibby Line* broke its crank axle at speed on an up West of England train near Crewkerne. The locomotive held the rails but the results could have been very much more serious. Visual inspection of other members of the class showed similar defects and 14 locomotives were immediately taken out of traffic while the rest were subject to ultrasonic testing; yielding five more possible failures. On 11th May the whole class was withdrawn from service pending replacement crank axles, resulting in a motive power crisis for the region. The light pacifics were also tested in the following months, but perhaps due to their lighter weight only a few locomotives were found to be defective. The crisis was answered by the other regions of BR with provision of seven Britannia's, seven black 5s, six V2 2-6-2s, 15 B1s and three BR standard class 5s on loan until the Merchant Navies began to return to traffic a few weeks' later. On 20th May 1953, V2 No.60896 of Doncaster shed departs promptly at 12.30pm with the down 'Bournemouth Belle', hauling the usual rake of wooden-bodied 12-wheeled Pullman cars. On the left may be seen Bulleid 2-set No. 69 at the rear of an up West of England train, with a gangwayed bogie luggage van at the end of a train in platform 11. The V2's were popular with South Western crews and proved very capable, if not quite the equal of a Merchant Navy. It is interesting to speculate on what Bulleid might have built had the Chief Civil Engineer not vetoed his original designs. We might have had 2-8-2s (like Gresley's P2 class) in place of the Merchant Navies and 2-6-2s (like Gresley's V2s) instead of the light pacifics. However, after the Sevenoaks accident of August 1927, George Ellson, then the newly appointed Chief Civil Engineer, always erred on the side of caution and this put an everlasting strain on relations between himself and successive Chief Mechanical Engineers. *RCR 4570*.

Taken the next day; 21st May 1953, we see ex-LMS diesel No. 10000, the tender of Britannia pacific No. 70029 *Shooting Star* (from the Western Region) and V2 No. 60917 from Kings Cross shed, the latter departing with a local to Salisbury comprising one of the 59ft Bulleid 3-sets and a van. Perhaps fortunately, the two LMS diesels were undergoing trials on the Southern at this time and could take a share of the traffic, along with Bulleid diesels Nos. 10201/2/3. No. 10000 is heading an Exeter train – so probably the time is either just before 1pm or 3pm as the Salisbury local would depart Waterloo at 54 minutes past the hour, just six minutes ahead of the express. It would be crossed to the local line at, probably, Hampton Court Junction, to keep it out of the way of the following service. Between the two, at 57 minutes past the hour, the regular Alton/Portsmouth electric (first stop Surbiton) and dividing at Woking would also depart – all trains routed via the down main. The motive power inspector's cabin is visible on the left; at the end of platform 11. Surprisingly, considering the interesting happenings, the usual band of spotters are not present. Maybe the inspector has tired of their presence and requested them to leave – well, words to that effect, anyway! *RCR 4581.*

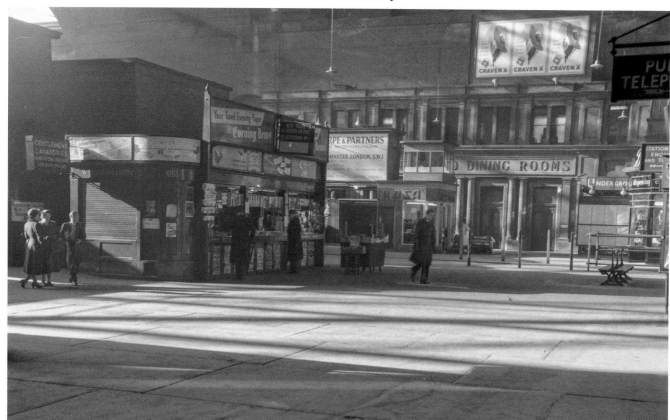

Opposite page: Two quiet views of Cannon Street station, taken on Tuesday, 9th November 1954 – presumably in the middle of the day. The station would be extremely busy during morning and evening rush hours, but could be almost deserted at other times and for many years was closed on Sundays. The first picture shows part of the concourse, with the ubiquitous W.H. Smith bookstall adorned with advertisements, newspapers and magazines to purchase for the journey, while the old refreshment rooms have clearly already dispensed their last meals. Note the "Next train to London Bridge" illuminated indicator above the bookstall. In the second picture we see a view across the buffer stops and the rather ramshackle barriers, with an ex-LBSCR 4-SUB electric unit standing in Platform 1. The equally rough metal canopies were provided as a prelude to the removal of the overall arched roof – damaged by bombing in the Second World War and never properly repaired. *RCR 5633/4.*

Above: The "country" end of Cannon Street station, taken just after the disastrous fire that destroyed most of the signal box early on the morning of 5th April 1957. The cause was an electrical short-circuit but it resulted in complete chaos on the South Eastern section for several days afterwards. For some time the station could only operate using hand signalling, severely limiting the services and all steam-hauled trains were diverted elsewhere. Special bus services also ran between Cannon Street and London Bridge stations for the benefit of commuters. Here the Hastings line steam set in platform 8 and the BR standard set in platform 7 were not going anywhere. Set 951 was a narrow 'Restriction 0' six-coach set at this time, formed of firsts 7419/20 in the centre, flanked by thirds (now seconds) 1029/30, with brake thirds (now seconds) 3672/74 at the ends. There were about 25 sets of Maunsell Hastings line stock – 8ft 0¾ in wide – built especially for the line between 1929 and 1934. Set numbers were 213-216, 475-480 and 937-951, although not all were in existence at the same time and they ranged from three to ten coaches each. On the day of the fire, the LM Region offered to supply a 225 lever power frame that was in store at Crewe. This was gladly accepted and part of was installed in the former staff rooms at the far end of the signal box (which had not been destroyed), coming into use on 5th May, allowing six of the eight platforms to be used. Construction of a new signal cabin began soon after – situated somewhat nearer to London Bridge but this did not open until December 1957. *RCR 10383.*

Chapter 3

Trains

Opposite: And here is the change at Cannon Street – taken on 12th June 1959. The overall roof has gone, there are alterations to the platform layout (with one platform less) and a diesel unit on the Hastings line service, although Bulleid 4-set 'Type N' No. 86 (now augmented to seven coaches) is alongside and will form a steam-hauled commuter express to Margate or Ramsgate. The site of the burnt-out signalbox is visible on the left, as is evidence of very recent track renewals with flat-bottomed rails. There is clearly some interest in the 6B type Hastings diesel unit as another photographer is also present, but Phase 1 of the Kent Coast electrification would be fully switched on in a matter of days and so there was plenty more to photograph. 6B unit No. 1033 was one of seven buffet-equipped (hence the classification) diesel units completed for the Hastings line service in 1958 – unit numbers being 1031-37. These joined the seven 6S (short) units numbered 1001-7 and twelve 6L (long) units numbered 1008-19 which had been completed in the previous two years. Motor coach S60037 is leading. The units proved harsh riders and most SR diesel-electrics ultimately received the nickname "Thumpers" which aptly described both the noise they made and their effect on the track. By this time they were BR classes 201, 202 and 203 respectively. *RCR 13609.*

This page: The down *Man of Kent* express passing through London Bridge station at just after 4.15pm on 13th March 1957, with West Country No. 34098 *Templecombe* in charge. This service was officially the 4.10pm down from Charing Cross to Margate via Folkestone and the 9.42am corresponding up train, but because the stock (usually two rakes formed of a BR standard Mk 1 3-set and about eight Bulleid coaches in green livery) were utilised on other trains, still with their roof boards in place, some observers considered that there were four daily workings. However, only the locomotives hauling the 9.42 up and 4.10 down carried headboards – which included the white horse emblem of Kent *"Invicta"* – and only these two ran non-stop between Waterloo East and Folkestone Central. This also gave a good subject for a pub quiz question; what separates a Kentish Man from a Man of Kent? The answer is the River Medway – anyone born west of the river is the former, anyone born east of it is the latter. In those days women of Kent did not seem to be mentioned – a situation that would not be tolerated today! For a Wednesday afternoon the platforms seem remarkably deserted – an hour later and they would certainly be crowded. *RCR 10328.*

Above: Battle of Britain No. 34085 *501 Squadron* arrives at Margate with a down special on 28th March 1959 – Easter Saturday. This locomotive had been a regular on the *Golden Arrow* and the three mounting brackets for the arrow may be seen on the side casing – but not so at this period as she is not in pristine condition. The original light pacifics could still be used on the train at this time – indeed the writer recalls seeing No. 34089 *602 Squadron* on the duty a year later on Easter Saturday 1960 – and the only time he saw the loco in original condition – but by then the rebuilt locomotives (usually Nos. 34088 and 34100) were preferred. No. 34085's train includes a SECR "Continental" brake third (now second) as the first vehicle – one of the Diagram 164A vehicles from the number range 3548-3559 – almost all of which would be withdrawn from service before the year was out. Behind the locomotive is the Southern Railway's monumental classic style station building of 1926, and now a Grade 2 listed building, attributed to SR architect Edwin Maxwell Fry. It is far better appreciated from the forecourt side. *RCR 13084.*

Opposite top*:* Ex-LBSCR station buildings were often lavish and extremely well-appointed – usually better than LSWR structures and almost always superior to SECR construction. This is the exterior of Denmark Hill on 5th April 1955. Built between 1864 and 1866 to the design of Charles Henry Driver, the station is situated on an overbridge spanning the four platforms and features an Italianate frontage with French pavilion-style roofs. For a period in the 1920s the waiting room was taken over by a religious sect and transformed with an altar and a colourful interior paint finish – note the "Assembly Hall" title on and over the nearest door. In March 1980 the then somewhat neglected building was set on fire and much of the roof was destroyed. British Rail set about demolition but were opposed by the Camberwell Society, who finally won the day and the building was restored five years later at a cost of £300K (about £900K in today's values) as a joint venture between BR and The Southwark Environment Trust. The restoration included a public house called, appropriately, The Phoenix. The area is said to have been named after Queen Anne's husband; Prince George of Denmark, who hunted in the area and had a country house built nearby. Note the various advertising hoardings outside. Along with the usual timetables and excursion publicity, the nearest poster features the Easter exhibition of the Model Railway Club, to be held at Central Hall, Westminster. Enthusiasts of a certain age will remember this popular annual event. *RCR 5705.*

Chapter 4

Stations and Scenes

This page, bottom: Southampton Terminus station on 24th June 1957, viewed looking towards the old docks from Central Bridge, which crossed the station throat and had replaced a previous rather inconvenient level crossing. Seen in the docks on the left is RMS Queen Mary, with Cunard cruise liner RMS Ivernia on the right. The station was built for the London & Southampton Railway in 1839 to the design of Sir William Tite and the roof may just be seen above M7 No. 30376 shunting an LMS van on the right. The larger building in the centre background is the Southampton Imperial Hotel – later the South Western Hotel and then office accommodation and this dates from 1872. The station was just plain Southampton until July 1858 when it became Southampton Docks, finally being renamed Terminus in July 1923. The layout seen dates from around 1891 and the two lines by-passing the station (between the signal posts) go across Canute Road and into the docks. On the left is part of the goods yard, with the extensive goods shed out of sight to the extreme left. In the station may be seen three trains of Bulleid stock – that on the left with a North Eastern Railway covered carriage truck on the rear having just arrived from, maybe Waterloo, Portsmouth, Reading, Salisbury or perhaps Bournemouth. The others visible are 3-sets Nos. 981 and 819, while to the right are a number of parcels vans – to where the M7 will probably shunt the crimson and cream-liveried vehicle. Closure of the station to passengers took place on 5th September 1966 and to freight traffic in December 1967. The site has been a car park since 1970 although both the station building (now a casino) and the hotel (now residential apartments) survive. Just one railway line crosses the site today, giving limited access to the docks. The signals are all SR upper quadrants – some mounted on rail-built main posts. Note also the LSWR water column on the right-hand platform. *RCR 10830.*

Opposite page: We now move around to Canute Road level crossing with two more views taken on 24th June 1957. In the first we see T9 No. 30313 crossing the road and signalled up the main line towards Northam. Here we are looking northwards towards Central Bridge, with Southampton Terminus station on the left and the large goods warehouse on the right. The enamelled sign "Goods Depot" may just be seen on the end wall, above the rather unhappy-looking flagman's head. He is equipped, not just with red flag but also with a bell. Another flagman may be seen to the left of the locomotive's tender and road traffic is clearly eager to resume its journey. In the second picture and turning through 180 degrees, the weather has clearly deteriorated as Feltham-allocated S15 No. 30499 reverses across the road into the docks, prior to picking up a perishables freight (most often meat or bananas) for Feltham and probably onwards to Nine Elms. These could load to a maximum of 70 wagons (including the brake van) but the S15s would have little difficulty handling them. In theory, all of Feltham's eight up goods reception roads could take a full load, but in fact not all did so and it was usual for the signalman at Staines West box to count the wagons and telephone forward advising of any up freight that exceeded 65 vehicles so enabling this to be routed into one of the longer sidings. *RCR 10827 and RCR 10824.*

This page: Continuing through the dock gates at Canute Road and turning right, a line of rails led to Southampton Town Pier and eventually, after 1933, through to the new docks. Part of this ran through the streets, where C14 class 0-4-0 tank No. 30588 (ex-LSWR No. 741/0741 and then SR No. 3741) is seen, but on 25th June 1957. Ten of these diminutive 2-2-0 "motor tanks" were built for pull-push working (with the LSWR "gate" stock coaches) in 1906-9, LSWR numbers being Nos. 736-745. They proved hopelessly inadequate and were later replaced by engines of classes 0415, O2, T1 and M7 on pull-push duties. Four of the motor tanks were rebuilt as conventional 0-4-0 tanks for light shunting duties and three, Nos. 741/44/45 became SR stock at the Grouping – the other seven being sold off by the LSWR during 1917. Eventually these became Southern numbers Nos. 3741, 3744 and departmental 77s – the latter being employed as the Redbridge sleeper works shunter. The other two operated over the town quay tramway until 1957, latterly carrying BR numbers 30588/89. Here the former looks extremely smart in the lined black livery applied in December 1952 and does not look like a candidate for withdrawal as occurred less than six months after being photographed. *RCR 10852.*

Opposite page: Moving up the line to Winchester City, earlier on 24th June 1957, BR standard mogul No. 76067 calls at the station with the much-delayed 6.35am Bournemouth West to Basingstoke stopper. Dick's notes tell us that the cause was a late running Ocean Liner express from Southampton which was given preference away from Allbrook, north of Eastleigh where four roads became two. On this occasion (as at Southampton), Dick took several colour pictures and his notes against these give some additional information not always recorded against the black & white views. The station was just plain Winchester until 1948, being renamed by BR to avoid confusion with the former Didcot, Newbury & Southampton Railway station at Chesil, on the other side of the city. On electrification in 1967, it returned to plain Winchester; Chesil by then having closed. In the sidings is a surprise visitor – ex-SECR P class 0-6-0 tank No. 31325 deputising for the more usual LSWR B4 shunter. Its shed accommodation (a sub-shed of Eastleigh) is visible just to the left of the P class – a corrugated sheet structure dating from 1928. A loco of this class was at Eastleigh for a few years in the late 1950s and they also occasionally appeared on the Havant-Hayling island branch instead of the usual LBSCR "terriers" – equally surprising. At neither location was the newcomer made to feel welcome! *RCR 10819.*

Above: Normality has returned to Winchester on 5th March 1960. Adams B4 dock tank No. 30093 shunts the yard alongside Winchester 'A' ground frame – a typical LSWR timber structure that housed a four-lever frame controlling the northern end of the up goods yard. Part of the yard at this location turned sharply to follow the Stockbridge Road valley and this necessitated a short-wheelbase shunting engine. The B4 tanks were found to be ideal and one was sub-shedded from Eastleigh for many years – until replaced by a 204hp diesel shunter in 1963. The class of 25 B4 tanks date from 1891 to 1908; the final five being built under Drummond's regime and differed in detail, sometimes being referred to as class K14. Fourteen were named and worked in Southampton Docks from 1893 onwards until replaced by USA tanks in 1947. No. 30093 was one of these and previously carried the name *St. Malo*. It was withdrawn soon after being photographed, after which the usual Winchester shunter became either No. 30096 or 30102. By this time just one other B4 remained in BR service – No. 30089 as shed pilot at Guildford. *RCR 14509.*

Privett station on the Meon Valley line, with the up "*Hampshireman*" enthusiast's special train hauled by T9s Nos. 30301 and 30732 passing through on a cold Sunday 6th February 1955. The local population have clearly turned out to see this final train pass through. The special followed a quite involved itinerary, leaving Waterloo for Guildford via Staines at 9.45am behind H2 Atlantic No. 32421. There a pair of LBSCR radial tanks took over for the run to Horsham (reverse) and then Petersfield via Cranleigh and Midhurst, where the two T9s took over for a rather circuitous return via Havant, Fareham, the Meon Valley line and on to Waterloo via Frimley, Sturt Lane Junction, Farnborough and Woking, arriving back there at just after 5pm. The Meon Valley was a rather odd line, running south through the hilly country from Alton to Fareham and was a late addition to the LSWR network, opening on 1st June 1903. Despite being engineered to main line standards, it was always treated as a minor branch line and after electrification to Alton in 1937 became the province of M7s and 2-coach pull-push sets, with virtually no through services. It had officially closed to passengers and through freight the day before this last special working. However, goods traffic continued until 1968 on truncated spurs south from Alton to Farringdon and north from Fareham as far as Droxford, the latter until 1962. At this location the station was then rented to The Sadler Rail Coach Company who were attempting to develop a rail-mounted road coach intended for branch line service. Nothing ultimately came of the invention and the whole venture petered out around 1970 following a certain amount of vandal damage. The writer made a couple of visits to Droxford in 1967/68 but it was obvious that visitors were not encouraged – presumably for that very reason. For a short time around this period it was also home to an embryonic locomotive preservation group. Although built as a single line but with engineering work able to take a second line of rails had this ever been needed, the route had originally featured passing loops at each of the stations. That at Privett was taken out of use in the 1920s leaving a long section from West Meon to Tisted and which explains why this up train is running on the down line. The former up platform line latterly in use as a goods siding. *RCR 5665.*

N15 class 4-6-0 No. 30787 *Sir Menadeuke*, built by North British Locomotive Company in September 1925 to Maunsell's design version of the class, arriving at Dorchester South from Weymouth on 10th July 1956 with a local service to Bournemouth. The train comprises a Maunsell corridor third in crimson lake and cream and a LSWR 58ft rebuilt 2-set – one of numbers 42-46. The picture was taken from the signal box which stood alongside the pointwork that gave access to the up platform and shows the unique layout very well. When the LSWR arrived here in June 1847 the company were expecting to progress westwards towards Bridport and Exeter, hence the station building was constructed at the side of the platforms to facilitate this extension. The GWR opened their line from Castle Cary to Weymouth ten years later and this effectively blocked any LSWR plans to go further – which would have involved some pretty heavy earthworks anyway. A curved connection was put in between this point and the GWR line, which with the construction of mixed gauge trackwork enabled the South Western to access Weymouth. A new down platform was built on the curve but up trains had to reverse into their platform before resuming their journey eastwards – a situation not remedied until as recently as June 1970. No. 30787 will proceed past the photographer and then set back into the platform road. Enamelled metal plates were set into the ballast alongside the up line, indicating to loco crews when to stop with the last coach clear of the points – these showing the number of coaches in the train. Like Winchester City, the station was just plain Dorchester until 1949, when the suffix "South" was added – the GWR station becoming Dorchester West. There was once an overall roof spanning the up platform and the three visible dead-end lines, but this was removed in 1938, together with another short platform serving the left-hand road. Note also the SR express bogie brake van just visible on the right – seen again on page 109. *RCR 7557.*

41

We will now take a trip down the West of England main line towards Exeter. The LSWR lines west of Exeter, known affectionately as "The Withered Arm" beyond is the subject of a separate book.

Opposite top: Original Merchant Navy No. 35003 *Royal Mail* runs into Andover Junction with a 12-coach train to the west and is about to pass Andover Junction East signal box, on Sunday 8th July 1956, so this is probably the 4pm to Plymouth. No. 35003 went new to Salisbury shed in September 1941, moving on to Exmouth Junction a year later, where she remained when transferred to Western Region stock on 1st January 1963 – having been rebuilt at Eastleigh between June and August 1959. Returned to the Southern Region in July 1964, she ended her days at Nine Elms in July 1967, having run some 1,131,793 miles. Of these almost 860,000 were in original condition – one of only five members of the class to record better annual utilisation before rebuilding than after. Read into that what you will but it is worth noting that the West of England route between Waterloo and Exeter would have given the best daily mileages for locomotives on the Southern. The signal box is a LSWR type 1 containing 50 levers and dates from the 1870s. *RCR 7496.*

Opposite bottom: However, just before we embark westwards, here for comparison is the first rebuilt Merchant Navy No. 35018 *British India Line*, standing in Waterloo platform 15, for inspection by BTC officials, 14th February 1956. Dick was clearly "in the know" for this. Opinion differed greatly as to whether the rebuilds were better locomotives – but they were certainly more economical and easier on maintenance. Just whether BR recouped the cost of rebuilding may also be debated, but when first rebuilt it was thought they would remain in service until circa 1975. Wishful thinking – or creative accounting? – but few individuals would have wanted to work in the conditions demanded by steam at that date. Prime Minister Harold Wilson's "white heat of technology" would have certainly left the steam locomotive behind by then. No. 35018 was new in May 1945, starting work from Nine Elms, where she remained for practically her entire life until withdrawn in August 1964, having run 956,544 miles (504,900 in original condition) and achieving better annual utilisation as a rebuild – the more usual situation. The loco was subjected to an extremely protracted overhaul following purchase for preservation and is currently on main line service, based at Carnforth. *RCR 5823.*

This page: Battle of Britain pacific No. 34069 *Hawkinge* calls at Yeovil Junction for water in the evening of 22nd July 1958 with a down freight. This view demonstrates the mixed traffic ability of the class, which was most often seen on the Salisbury-Exeter route, although the propensity of the Bulleids for slipping caused many a crew concern on wet days. The loco was new in October 1947 – one of six named after airfields involved in the Battle of Britain – in this case situated inland from Folkestone. Appropriately first allocated to Ramsgate shed, she moved to Stewarts Lane in December 1949, moving west to Exmouth Junction in March 1954. Not renowned as one of the better performers of the class, the loco was withdrawn in November 1963 – one of the first ten to be taken out of traffic and was cut up at Eastleigh Works during May 1964. Another Bulleid may just be seen in the distance, beyond the footbridge. Yeovil Junction station is now a shadow of its former self with just the left-hand island platform now used for trains. However, beyond the right-hand island platform the Yeovil Railway Centre now has its headquarters and operates steam and diesel days regularly through the year. They also have a collection of rolling stock including a couple of wagons of Southern Railway origin. *RCR 12457.*

Above: Yeovil Junction station is actually situated in the village of Stoford, about two miles south of the town. In steam days it was connected to Yeovil Town station by a pull-push shuttle train service and this is seen here approaching the Junction propelled by M7 0-4-4 tank no. 30129 on 10th July 1959. The "gate" set is no. 373 – the final survivor of a rather distinctive group of LSWR coaches. The original idea behind this stock was to mirror the competing street trams, hence the open interiors and gated vestibules to the compartments. Some coaches had begun life as steam railmotors in the 1903-6 period and were later rebuilt, others such as set 373 were built new for pull-push working. Trailing the locomotive is the through coach for Waterloo – a Maunsell brake composite – and this will be taken onwards to Salisbury by a stopping train perhaps hauled by the mogul whose tender is just visible on the right, beyond Yeovil Junction A signal box, which dates from 1909. Note complete absence of headcode disc on the front of the PP set – not that anyone would be confused about the destination. *RCR 13817.*

Opposite: Conveyance of milk featured large in traffic from the West of England to London and was shared between the Great Western and the Southern. On the latter there were depots at Torrington, Lapford, Crediton, Seaton Junction, Chard Junction, Sherborne, Semley and on the S&DJR line, the milk from which travelled to London overnight, with corresponding return empty tank workings on the following day. Several dairy companies were involved and that at Chard Junction was originally Wiltshire Dairies – later part of the United Dairies empire. They employed this diminutive Ruston 0-4-0 diesel locomotive to shunt the milk tanks at Chard, seen on 23rd July 1958, freshly repainted in UD black livery with white lettering. The former ownership lettering may just be seen below the UD logo. The loco was still there in 1974, by which time it had been joined by a second more modern Ruston diesel in bright yellow livery. Rail-borne general milk traffic ceased in 1980, but there was a brief revival in August 1981, by which time just the bright yellow diesel loco remained. The dairy itself continued to function, served by road transport, until 2015 and the buildings were demolished a year later. A similar Ruston diesel, numbered DS1169 was employed at the Broad Clyst permanent way depot. *RCR 12463.*

Some of the celebrated survivors in the West of England were the three Adams radial tanks used on the Lyme Regis branch until 1961. Here No. 30582 departs from Axminster station (seen in the background) with a single LSWR brake composite coach for Lyme Regis on 10th July 1956. The loco is just passing the branch home signal – a Southern lattice-mast upper quadrant with a Westinghouse shunt disc mounted low down on the post. The train is climbing up to cross the bridge over the main line (bridge No. 444C) before turning south to head for Combpyne (the only intermediate station on the branch) and Lyme Regis. Although Axminster station was well-situated for the town centre, that at Lyme Regis most certainly was not – and definitely not for the beach – the result, was that closure was inevitable, which took place on 29th November 1965. The track and most structures stood intact until the spring of 1967, enabling South Western Circle founder member Ted (A. E.) West to walk the entire line photographing practically every aspect. He intended to model Lyme Regis station in 7mm scale – a dream that was sadly never to be realised. RCR 7577.

Top: The peace of Seaton Junction is disturbed by No. 34109 *Sir Trafford Leigh Mallory* as it snakes its way through the station, Waterloo bound on 11th July 1959 with the 9.40 from Ilfracombe. The three leading coaches (Maunsell 2nd, open 2nd and restaurant car) plus the loco have come from Exeter Central. *RCR 13840.*

Bottom: A short time later the up 8.30 Padstow-Waterloo, including through coaches from Bude, departs for Waterloo hauled by No. 35008 *Orient Line*, from Exmouth Junction shed. The loco, together with Maunsell 1936 3-set 960, the restaurant, dining car and possibly the sixth coach have all been added at Exeter Central, while the Bulleid 59ft 3-set and the four Maunsells on the rear have come up from Cornwall. This 13-coach train would be the normal maximum load allowed into Waterloo and would have to be routed into either platform 10 or 11, or, by special arrangement, into platform 14 (it would block platform 15 while standing there). The magnificently tall LSWR bracket signal may be sighted from afar above the footbridges and includes repeaters at a lower level for trains stopping at the station. Note also the through lines have been re-laid with flat-bottom rail. The station closed along with the Seaton branch on 7th March 1966 and today the place is a scene of dereliction, with just a single through line passing the deserted and overgrown platforms. The station has been the subject of several models over the years, including a 2mm scale one that once graced Pecorama at Beer, however it is currently the subject of a new 4mm scale layout being constructed by Southampton Model Railway Society – and will eventually be seen at exhibitions. *RCR 13839.*

Opposite top: BR standard 3 2-6-2 tank No. 82010 arriving at Sidmouth on 13th October 1959, with a train from Sidmouth Junction – or perhaps a "short" working from Tipton St. Johns, the junction for the line to Budleigh Salterton and Exmouth. The train comprises a Maunsell brake composite and a BR standard 10-compartment non-corridor second – one of those built for Exeter-Exmouth line services and delivered from Swindon Works in late 1955. The Maunsell is therefore likely to be in BR green livery, the second in BR crimson lake. The BR standard tanks were replacements for M7 tanks in the Exeter area and appeared there in 1953. Sidmouth as a resort strove to be rather select (it remains so today) and the station was sited a mile or so inland and somewhat above the centre of the town. It lost its passenger service on 6th March 1967, goods two months later. The station buildings, goods shed and former engine shed at Sidmouth survive in alternative uses, but the rather picturesque signal box does not. Unfortunately, signal boxes were a rather specialised form of railway building that do not lend themselves to alternative uses. This is a LSWR type 1 box but was not the original built for the opening in 1874 – that was situated behind the photographer near the engine shed. Possibly the old upper (timber) storey was re-used on a new brick base in about 1905? Note that there is a cantilevered extension on the far end of the structure. *RCR 14372.*

Opposite bottom: Moving westwards along the coast, the next branch was to Exmouth. This was a true commuter line and for this reason is still with us today, marketed as The Avocet Line. Unfortunately the extensive 4-platform station constructed by the Southern Railway in 1924 and seen here viewed from the signal box is not and was replaced by a single platform and new somewhat minimalist (but better than some modern stations) brick-built structure in 1976. In this all-action picture from 12th October 1959, a BR standard 2-6-2 tank is just leaving Platform 4 on the left for Tipton St. Johns and Sidmouth Junction, while another loco of the same class is shunting down onto its train for Exeter Central in Platform 2. The latter is formed of BR Mk 1 non-corridor 3-set 153 (one of four such sets allocated to the line) while the other train consists of a Southern Railway Van B complete with "newspapers" roof boards, a Maunsell corridor brake composite and a SECR 60ft ten-compartment second – so is one of the West Country 2-sets type W numbered between 100 and 110. A few years earlier and the locomotives would have all been M7 0-4-4 tanks, although the photographer did record at least one member of the class here during his October 1959 visit. Even at this late date the platform starting signals are all still LSWR lower quadrants. The signal box was provided with a balcony at the station end to facilitate token collection and this is where Dick is standing to take his picture. The goods yard, containing more spare coaches, is seen on the right while the small single-road engine shed may just be seen above the SECR coach, behind the starting signal. *RCR 14362.*

This page: Z class 0-8-0 shunter No. 30956 is seen at Exmouth Junction marshalling yard on 16th July 1958, coupled to shunting truck S61322 – whose companion S61323 was seen previously at Clapham Yard. Whilst passenger traffic on the Southern in the west was concentrated on Exeter Central, locomotive and goods facilities were centred on Exmouth Junction – a couple of miles to the east. A single example of the Z class (usually No. 30954) was allocated to Exmouth Junction shed for many years and was employed shunting the marshalling yard there. In February 1956 Nos. 30950/56 were sent westwards with a view to replacing the ageing ex-LBSCR E1R tanks on banking duties between St David's and Central stations, however the Western Region refused to sanction their use until August 1959. After this, all eight locomotives of the class appeared at Exmouth Junction until replaced by W class tanks in 1962 – a move most definitely not approved of by footplate crews. *RCR 12291.*

Above: At Exmouth Junction shed on 29th August 1954, West Country pacific No. 34021 *Dartmoor* is surrounded by other pacifics – with prototype Merchant Navy No. 35001 *Channel Packet* immediately to the left. Exmouth Junction had a large number of Bulleids allocated – sometimes as many as eight Merchant Navies and 35 light pacifics and in later years held a concentration of the unmodified examples since neither the North Devon or the North Cornwall lines were ever cleared for the rebuilt engines. No. 34021 was new in January 1946, going first to Ramsgate but migrating to Exmouth Junction in July 1947, moving further west to Plymouth Friary in April 1948 – one of just five reallocated there at the time. She returned to Exmouth Junction in late 1950, remaining there until rebuilt in December 1957. A stint on the Eastern section followed before returning to the Western section in 1961 where the loco powered the last up steam-hauled Southampton boat train into Waterloo on 9th July 1967 – being photographed at both Canute Road and on arrival at Waterloo on that momentous day. The loco then ran light to Salisbury to await the call to the South Wales scrapyards – in this case Cashmore's of Newport where cutting up was reported in March 1968. *RCR 5298.*

Opposite: We leave the line beyond Exeter just as the 11am up Padstow to Waterloo service joins the GWR main line at Cowley Bridge Junction on 28th August 1954, behind light pacific No. 34023 *Blackmore Vale.* For the couple of miles into St David's, the train will be running on the down Western Region line – an anomaly which was also repeated further west at Plymouth North Road station. This 10-coach load should receive the services of two banking engines coupled to the rear of the train up the 1 in 37 to Exeter Central – most likely to be a pair of E1R tanks. Bulleid 5-set 849 is leading, followed by either a Maunsell buffet car or open third, a Bulleid open third and a Bulleid 59ft 3-set on the rear – all in "blood and custard" livery. On this day, the whole train will have originated at Padstow. Those were the days!! *RCR 5278.*

Chapter 6

Rolling Stock

A somewhat unlikely coach to be seen at Wadebridge, this is ex-LNWR 12-wheeled sleeping car DM198932 in the siding beyond the turntable, on 12th July 1960. Built in 1903 for West Coast Joint Line services, it became an LMS departmental vehicle during World War 2 – probably also for temporary staff sleeping accommodation during those difficult times. In 1949 it and four others passed to the Southern Region motive power department who used them as dormitory accommodation for staff during the summer period. Another was DM198930 at Lyme Regis – with the others noted at Seaton, Bude and Launceston but it is possible that they moved about. Such additional sleeping accommodation for staff during the summer season was necessary when considerably more trains would start and end up at West of England branch line locations. Staff would either need to be there early, particularly on Saturday mornings for the up trains or might find themselves similarly placed after working a down train in the evening hence such provision was probably cheaper than offering them overnight hotel accommodation – which in high season was probably expensive and fully-booked anyway. Such things were usually provided with good financial reason – for the company!! Withdrawal is recorded as June 1965. *RCR 15039.*

There were few true Southern Railway vehicles that ran on 12 wheels. This is the former LBSCR Director's saloon DS291, seen at Stewarts Lane sidings on 26th May 1958. It still carries crimson lake and cream livery, with left-hand end numbering – the only ex-Brighton coach to be painted in these colours after 1948. Construction began at Lancing Works in 1914 but was halted by wartime pressures and was not completed until four years later. Designed by Albert Harry Panter, it was painted in lined umber livery, numbered LBSCR 60 and kept at Brighton Works for use only by the "top brass". As there was no separate Guard's compartment, It normally ran coupled to 6-wheeled passenger brake van No. 380 – maintained in equally pristine condition. Once in Southern Railway ownership it was repainted olive green and "re-allocated" to Longhedge (Stewarts Lane), carrying the departmental number 291s; continuing to be used only for special official visits. Some rebuilding of windows and the fitting of gangway connections took place in 1934. Being kept under cover, it retained its original BR two-tone livery until November 1962, then receiving Southern Region green. Withdrawn in early 1965, its historical importance as the last ex-LBSCR coach in mainland service was acknowledged and it was offered to the BRB curator of historic relics for preservation. However, it was refused and sold to the Bluebell Railway instead, arriving there on 4th August 1965. There it was used, mostly on Sunday afternoon tea trains until about 1970, after which it was taken out of service. Since then it has at least been stored under cover and the intention is to return it to original condition. However, estimates for this exceed £100K, even with the help of volunteer labour, so with its somewhat limited use capabilities, it remains low on the restoration priorities list. *RCR 11849.*

Above: The ex-LSWR Director's saloon, DS1, at Faversham on 20th March 1959, in use for crew-training and route learning procedures in preparation for electrification, on this day it was being propelled by H class tank No. 31512, which has gone to the loco shed for servicing. The coach is painted lined crimson lake livery – the livery which it carried until withdrawal in April 1963. Built as long ago as 1885, it was much rebuilt during its long career, including being mounted on a second hand (but newer) underframe in 1950. Perhaps not as imposing as the LBSCR saloon, but probably as well-appointed internally. Its replacement on the Southern Region was converted Maunsell coach DS70155. *RCR 13049.*

Opposite top: A very slightly more ordinary LSWR vehicle – in this case a 46ft 6in invalid saloon on the Longmoor Military Railway on 30th April 1966 – the occasion of the second special train to visit the line hauled by WD 2-10-0 No. 600 *Gordon*. The writer was on the first tour a fortnight earlier – in pouring rain!! The stock from the special may be seen in the background. Coach WD3007 was part of Longmoor's VIP train – the other coaches being a SECR saloon and an LNWR 6-wheeled saloon with open-ended balconies – all being maintained in immaculate dark blue livery. The LSWR vehicle dates from November 1910 – one of a pair – LSWR No. 11, later 4105 in the 1912 renumbering scheme. It became SR No. 7803 to Diagram 581 and was sold to the military in February 1938 – subsequently carrying several different Army numbers. It originally had gangways (removed after 1938) and lasted to closure of the Longmoor Military Railway in October 1969, going first to the Severn Valley Railway and later to the Kent & East Sussex Railway. Regrettably, since arriving there very little restoration has taken place and the coach no longer looks in the fine condition depicted here. Very considerable amounts of work will be needed to return it to passenger-carrying service. If the photographer stood in this location today, he would be in the middle of the southbound carriageway of the A3 trunk road! *RCR 17935.*

Opposite bottom: Taken on the same day, this is an ex-LSWR dining car now running as Army AD3019, standing in the yard area which was at a slightly lower level than Longmoor Downs station. A total of 23 of these dining cars were built by the LSWR – 19 with the window arrangement seen here and four more with larger single panes in place of the three smaller ones at each seating bay in the saloons. The kitchen area was amidships, where the corridor section and double doors are situated. As built they all had clerestory roofs and came to the Southern Railway as Diagram 590, SR numbers being 7821-43 (the final four with larger windows). Between 1931 and 1935 they were all rebuilt – the clerestory roof being replaced by the elliptical profile seen here, while some were altered internally to become open saloon vehicles instead of dining cars – four different diagrams then being allocated. This particular coach was LSWR No. 76, completed in 1908. It became No. 4138 in the 1912 renumbering scheme and later SR No. 7838. Rebuilt as

an unclassed saloon with the new roof profile in May 1931, it was then allocated to SR Diagram 593. Like most of its sisters, it was transferred to military use during World War 2 – in this case as US ambulance car 202 based at Netley in October 1943, finding its way to Longmoor (along with two others) by about 1950 and moving later to the Bicester Military Railway. It arrived on the Mid-Hants Railway in 1978 but little restoration was carried out there and the coach changed ownership a number of times, ending up on the Pontypool & Blaenavon Railway in 1993. Here some restoration was completed but its present status is unknown. The vehicle to the left is one of the former SR utility vans converted to Army workshop vans during World War 2, many of which travelled to the Continent from late 1944 onwards. These two Longmoor photographs are the most recent in the book and Dick's own register only lists another 50 or so black and white pictures taken down to July 1967 – after which only some colour slides were taken.
RCR 17930/35.

Above: Already bearing the mark of condemnation, ex-SECR saloon No. S7919S is seen at Eardley Road sidings (Streatham) on 30th October 1960, having been withdrawn during the previous September. It carries crimson lake and cream livery – one of few SECR Wainwright era coaches to be so finished. Built in 1905 by Metropolitan, it was one of three slightly different first class saloons completed then for Royal Train duties – although this coach was sometimes used for other special traffic, and was numbered SECR 3785. It was allocated to SR Diagram 618 and in March 1937 authority was given for it to be converted into an invalid saloon. However there appears to have been no urgency to this until the sale of two other invalid saloons to the Longmoor Military Railway in 1938 and the work was not actually completed until January 1939. The coach then assumed the appearance as seen. In the 1950s it was much used for Lourdes pilgrim traffic, eventually being replaced on these duties by four converted Maunsell coaches. By April 1960 it was noted at Gatwick Airport sidings, en route to Newhaven for breaking up. *RCR 15469.*

Opposite top: Two ex-SECR post office vans at Rotherhithe Road carriage sidings on 31st July 1958. Both differ slightly in detail. No. 4950 in the centre of the picture was to SR Diagram 1204 and was built as a GPO van, complete with lavatory facilities, No. 4955 on the right was to Diagram 1207 – built originally as a luggage van but converted to GPO use in 1931, then receiving the provision of a lavatory, although the differences are not very apparent in the photograph. Both vans are 50ft 1in long and date from 1906/7. They were amongst a small group of South Eastern vans used on mail trains from either Victoria or London Bridge to Dover and Folkestone, although there was a service between Holborn Viaduct and Newhaven during Southern Railway days. Both were withdrawn during 1960 when the remaining Dover service was taken over by a combination of more modern Maunsell vehicles and some other GPO vans imported from other regions. Through the open door the row of desks and mail racks that ran along the entire far side of the van may just be seen. Note also the provision of a very large dynamo under van 4950 – as the trains ran at night this was essential. Unlike some GPO vans on other regions, these never carried the bright red post office livery and remained green (of whatever shade) during BR ownership. *RCR 12537.*

Opposite bottom: A more typical ex-SECR "birdcage" coach, photographed awaiting breaking up at Newhaven on 18th March 1951. SR No. 3306 was a 50ft 1in example of SR Diagram 149 – having four third class compartments and a pair of lavatories accessible only from the middle two compartments, a large luggage van and brake compartment – the latter with the raised roof lookout. It was built in July 1908 (SECR No. 964) for general SECR services and after 1923 ran at one end of SR sets 690, then 662 and finally 912 – the latter set number being visible on the coach end. This last was a 9-coach formation used mostly for excursion and special traffic – an identical coach 3311 (seen behind) was at the other end of the set. Withdrawal is recorded as March 1951 – so little time was lost in sending the set for breaking up. The livery is faded and flaking SR malachite green with Bulleid-style insignia. Note the "flooring" and walkway in the foreground – built using parts from broken up goods wagons. Remember, the Southern never wasted anything! *RCR 4228.*

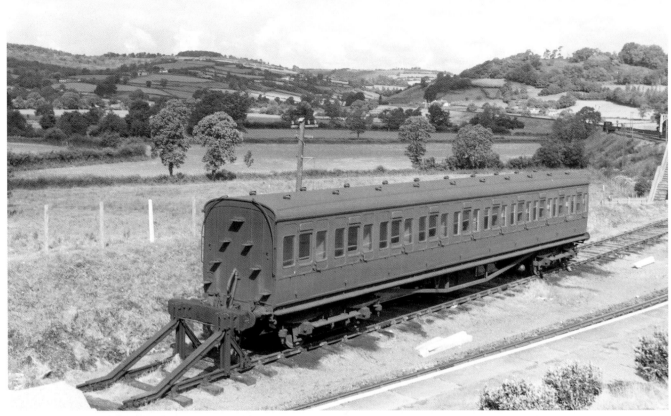

A SECR coach in crimson lake livery (not that this is very apparent here but Dick also took a colour slide) against the verdant green scenery of East Devon. The unique "pattern or prototype splicing coach" No. 1050 is parked in the sidings at Seaton Junction on 24th July 1958 – serving as the spare pull-push coach for the Seaton branch train. The main line towards Exeter may be seen climbing away from the junction above the coach, following the valley of the Umborne Brook (a tributary of the River Axe) towards Honiton tunnel. This coach was built as a trial run for the many electric stock conversions produced by the Southern from 1925 onwards. The underframe was to a unique length – 62ft 5in over headstocks – and was completed at Lancing some time in 1924. It was then sent to Ashford for mounting of bodywork – which involved all five compartments from 6-wheeled first SECR No. 792 (those at the left-hand end) plus three compartments from third No. 568 (those at the right-hand end). The remaining two compartments may have come from a second class coach or may have been built new simply to fill the gap in the middle – probably the latter. For accounting purposes the coach was allocated the number 1440 – in the SECR series and following on from the last 60ft "long ten" (see next picture) which carried the SECR number 1437. Having completed the body and any snags ironed out, the vehicle was set aside and similar electric stock conversions then took priority. Three years later, and having an almost complete coach in the workshops, attention was again turned to No. 1440 and in April 1927 it was outshopped as a composite, numbered SR 5546, with four 1st class and six 3rd class compartments, allocated SR Diagram 319 – unique in almost every respect. For a while it was placed in "birdcage" 3-set 528, later in unique 3-set 760 allocated to Maidstone West-Paddock Wood services. In July 1943 it was downgraded to all-third and renumbered 1050, to Diagram 50, pull-push through-piped and reallocated to the South Western section. It then served at Seaton, Lymington and Swanage before withdrawal in December 1962. It was then sent to the Ardingly "dump" of condemned coaches, from where it was rescued by the Bluebell Railway in May 1963. There it was "restored" to SECR No. 1050 and painted in lake livery and was much used until the early 1970s, when it was withdrawn pending a much more extensive restoration. This has yet to take place at the time of writing but the vehicle is at least now stored under cover at Horsted Keynes. *RCR 12478.*

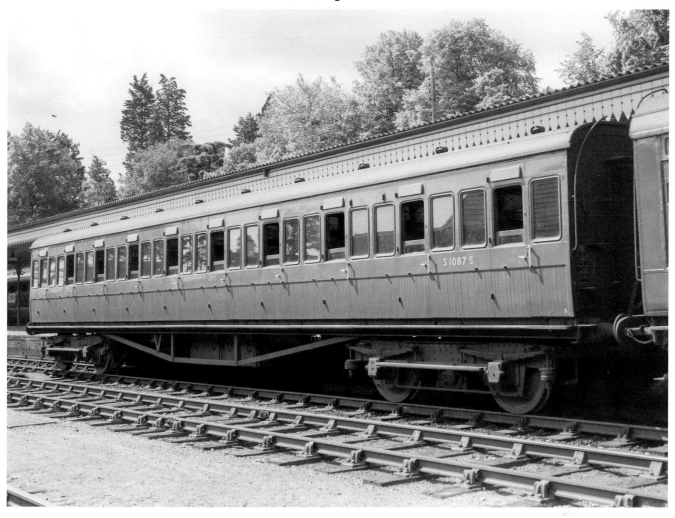

A SECR "long ten" – 60ft 1in ten compartment third (now second) No. 1087 at Sidmouth on 24th July 1958 – also wearing crimson lake livery and (we know from a separate image) coupled to Maunsell corridor brake composite No. 6594 (in green livery) forming 2-set W No. 109. This coach is one of just ten to feature matchboarded bodywork below the waistline (SR Nos. 1084-93) – the remaining 56 examples to Diagram 52 were steel-panelled. Built at Ashford in April 1922, on an underframe supplied by Birmingham RCW Co., as SECR No. 1405, it was repainted in SR olive green livery on 21st March 1929 (a fairly late repaint) and ran mostly on South Eastern section services apart from a spell in West London line set 98 between 1944 and 1947. West of England 2-set 109 was formed in 1958, but coach No. 1087 was replaced in the set by a Maunsell open third soon after being photographed and the coach returned eastwards, to be withdrawn in December 1959 and incorporated into the Lancing Works staff train, renumbered as departmental DS70064. It was finally retired from this duty in November 1963. *RCR 12481.*

Above: With the exception of pull-push sets, ex-LBSCR steam-hauled coaches became a rare sight on the mainland after about 1942 but continued to run on the Isle of Wight until the end of steam in December 1966. There were a number of different types – some unaltered from their mainland state, others extensively rebuilt. 54ft six-compartment brake third No. S4154 was one of those hardly altered for Island use – apart from removal of the side lookouts (which would have taken place sometime between 1927 and 1930), steel panelling has replaced the timber mouldings. This particular example began life as LBSCR No. 649 in 1916 – one of 18 such vehicles. Renumbered as SR 4027 after 1923 and allocated to Diagram 203, it ran at one end of 3-coach set 763 until 1936. Renumbering and transfer to the Isle of Wight took place in May 1936, after which the coach was allocated to Ryde-Cowes 3-set 488 for a number of years. The Isle of Wight diagram number was 210. Isle of Wight set formations tended to be rather fluid, especially after 1950 and by 25th June 1957, the date of the photograph, No. 4154 was painted crimson lake and included in Ryde-based Ventnor line set 495. By 1964 the coach had been fully steel-sheeted but was withdrawn in January 1966 – just failing to last until the end of steam working. Beyond is ex-SECR rebuilt composite S6377. The van body on the right is also of interest. Unique ex-LSWR 26ft fruit train brake van LSWR No. 46 dates from 1895. It was renumbered as LSWR van 4362 in 1913 and SR van No. 1 after the Grouping. Transferred to the Isle of Wight in May 1930, it then became SR No. 1007 and was withdrawn from service in June 1938. Then grounded (well – actually mounted on timber baulks spanning a trackside stream!) it remained in use as a store until about 1965. *RCR 10839.*

Opposite bottom: Ex-LBSCR passenger luggage vans were mostly six-wheeled and 30ft long – and were an equally rare sight after 1942 – although quite a number remained in departmental service beyond that date. This is former "Grande Vitesse" ventilated van SR 2116, seen on the quayside at Newhaven on 12th July 1950, still showing traces of its former SR lettering. However, this forms the subject of a minor mystery. No. 2116 is listed in Southern Railway registers as a Diagram 975 ordinary luggage van – like the one now preserved on the Bluebell Railway and not a ventilated fruit van, and was withdrawn in June 1940, to become a stores van (still on its wheels) at Newhaven. So, at least that part of the story seems right. Diagram 978 was the correct diagram for the van in the photograph and one of these, SR No. 2174, is listed as becoming departmental 1625s in August 1941 but this appears as a Diagram 975 luggage van. The two vehicles must have swapped identities at some point, presumably some time before departmental conversion, as this van clearly displays the traffic department number 2116. Such changes of identity were not unknown – but would only be apparent to a railway enthusiast. The exact Brighton origin of either van therefore cannot be stated with certainty. *RCR 4087*.

This page: Ex-LSWR "trailer brake composite" No. 6557 is seen at Callington – terminus of the former PD&SWJR branch from Bere Alston – on 30th August 1954. This was one of an interesting small group of vehicles – rebuilds of the steam railmotors that had been introduced early in the 20th century to try to compete with street trams and the forerunners of the "gate" stock pull-push set No. 373 seen at Yeovil Junction in an earlier picture. The first steam railmotors were those for the joint LSWR/LBSCR East Southsea branch and were introduced in 1903. They were followed by 15 more LSWR examples (of two types) and others introduced by several more railway companies in the following years. None were particularly successful and the LSWR examples were rebuilt as open vestibule coaches between 1916 and 1922. Twelve became SR Diagram 415, SR numbers being 6548-59, after 1923, and were originally equipped with the LSWR 3-wire pull-push gear. This also proved less than reliable and was replaced by compressed air control in 1929/30, but only one of the railmotor rebuilds (No. 6556) was so fitted. The rest became loose coaches at various locations on the South Western section but because of their unusual construction features (mostly regarding the trellis-type entrance gates) tended to be kept at certain specific locations. Weymouth and the Plymouth area saw them more often than most and by the 1950s coaches 6557/8 were often running as a pair on the Callington branch until withdrawn together in April 1956. However, on this day, they were running separately. The former driver's compartment – with three end windows, is nearest the camera. Also visible is the bunker of LMS Ivatt 2-6-2 tank No. 41315, which on that day was sharing the branch duties with O2 No. 30236. Behind, and only just seen, is former MOY 13-ton 7-plank private owner coal wagon P102220 . *RCR 5338.*

Opposite top: Bentley station, on 12th September 1954 with M7 No. 30328 and LSWR pull-push set 32 on the Bordon branch service. This was a somewhat unusual survivor – a steam-worked branch inside the electrified area, but clearly the traffic on the branch was insufficient (or at least fluctuated too much in nature) for it to ever be included in Southern Railway electrification plans. The branch diverged from the line to Alton a few yards south of Bentley signal box – seen in the background. Set No. 32 comprised 56ft driving brake third 3055, and 58ft rebuilt composite 4745 while the spare coach (just seen at left) was another 58ft rebuild; composite No. 4648. The latter is certainly lined crimson lake – the pull-push set probably unlined crimson. The branch closed to passengers on 16th September 1957 but remained open for regular goods traffic to and from the northern terminus of the Longmoor Military Railway until 4th April 1966. From time to time during the goods -only era special troop trains and the occasional enthusiast's special would be seen on the branch. *RCR 5513.*

Opposite bottom: Similar pull-push sets Nos. 36 and 31 sandwich M7 No. 30110 on an SLS enthusiast's special at Bishops Waltham, 3rd May 1953 – a much photographed event at the time. The Bishops Waltham branch ran northwards from Botley on the Eastleigh-Fareham line but was never particularly profitable. It opened amidst high hopes on 1st June 1863 and closed to passengers as long ago as 31st December 1932. Several northerly extensions were proposed in the early days, but none were ever realised. Goods traffic continued until 27th April 1962, latterly only twice or three times each week. During the goods-only era a few enthusiast specials visited the line and this one ran from Gosport (depart 1.20pm) to Fareham, Botley, Bishops Waltham (reverse) and back to Botley, Fareham and Havant, terminating at 3.30pm. The locomotive is taking water during the 35 minute layover at the branch terminus. Evidence of a reasonable level of goods traffic may be seen and this only really declined after 1958. Pull-push set 36 comprised LSWR 56ft driving brake third 3070 and 58ft rebuilt composite 4749, both in immaculate lined crimson lake livery. Set 31 (seen in the distance) was in a similar livery. *RCR 4506.*

This page: The Railway Enthusiast's Club *Compass Rose* rail tour at Ash Green station on 5th October 1957, hauled by M7 No. 30051 with ex-LBSCR pull-push set 721 in tow. Dick was a participant on the trip and also took several colour pictures – which tells us that the pull-push set was painted unlined crimson lake. The trip began at Farnborough station and made a circuitous tour of branches in Surrey, Hampshire and Berkshire before terminating again at Farnborough. Included were visits to Godalming Goods, Reading Central Goods, Thorneycroft's siding (Basingstoke), Aldershot Government sidings and the Tongham branch – on which Ash Green station was situated. This picture was taken during the ten minute stop, recorded as being from 2.56 to 3.06pm. The line through Ash Green was opened by the LSWR in 1849, on their route from Guildford to Farnham – extended to Alton three years later. Once the direct main line cut off from Woking through Aldershot to Farnham opened in 1870 the line became a backwater, was singled in 1930 and passenger traffic ceased in 1937, upon electrification of other surrounding routes. The section from Tongham to Farnham Junction was closed and severed at the western end on 21st November 1954. Goods traffic to Tongham gasworks continued until 31st December 1960 but the track remained in-situ for a number of years afterwards. Today, the station building is a private house. *RCR 11315.*

Opposite top: A better view of an ex-LBSCR pull-push set, this time leaving Tonbridge for Tunbridge Wells West and propelled by H class tank No. 31554, on 19th April 1958. Set 729 comprises driving brake third (now second) No. 3826 and composite No. 6202. Both date from 1911 and were previously LBSCR Nos. 1344 and 641 respectively. They were originally intended for services between Brighton and Worthing. No set number was allocated in Brighton days but after 1923 the pair became SR set 996. The set was recorded as being allocated to Epsom Downs by 1924, Eastbourne by 1931, Brighton in 1935 but simply "Central section" thereafter. It was renumbered as set 729 in 1937 to clear the set number range 980-999 for additional electric stock trailer sets then being converted, which were numbered in descending order from 1000. Withdrawal came in June 1960. Note that entry to the guard's/driver's compartment is by a large sliding door on each side – also that no sign of a driver is visible! The impressive up home signals are also noteworthy – eight arms including a shunt arm located on the main post. *RCR 11665.*

Opposite bottom: On the face of it, this shows ex-LBSCR pull-push set No. 726 on the rear of an up Exeter to Salisbury stopping train at Axminster on 11th July 1959. However, all is not quite what it seems. Driving brake third (now second) 3821 is present, but the other coach of the set, composite 6245 is not – having been withdrawn from service in June 1957. Its place has been taken by a LSWR 58ft rebuilt third to SR Diagram 31 whose identity is not known for certain, but vehicle 253 is a likely contender – this latter coach was not pull-push equipped so the pair are being used as normal loco-hauled stock. Both were seen running together at locations as diverse as Barnstaple, Exeter, Portsmouth and Eastleigh during the summer of 1959 and both were withdrawn together in the following October. The livery of each was recorded as unlined crimson lake. *RCR 13835.*

Below: Two ex-LSWR coaches at Evercreech Junction on 22nd July 1958. Each are October 1936 rebuilds on SR standard 58ft underframes and both began life as identical 48ft composites. The origin of the nearest coach, brake third No. 2626, is the easiest to identify. The six passenger compartments, plus the two pairs of lavatories farthest from the camera constitute the original vehicle, while the nearest 10ft steel-sheeted section forming the guard's van was added in the 1936 rebuilding. SR Diagram 98 was then allocated. Composite No. 4654 beyond was more extensively rebuilt, having the original body split into two sections and mounted at each end of the new underframe. One pair of lavatories was dismantled and two third class compartments fitted into the resultant gap of about 13ft 6in. SR Diagram 285 was then allocated. Both coaches were allocated to the S&DJR for relief work from 1954, remaining so allocated until withdrawn in July 1959 – by then some of the last ex-LSWR coaches in service – albeit perhaps not very often. Their livery remains SR malachite green, but with BR *Gill Sans* lettering, so neither coach has been repainted during their final ten years or so – probably just a revarnishing or two. *RCR 12448.*

Chapter 7

Out on the Line

This page: The roofs of Brighton surround us here with a view along the Lewes Road viaduct on the Kemp Town branch; this and the following two pictures were taken on 23rd August 1952. This wholly urban railway was opened on 2nd August 1869, to serve the eastern side of the Brighton conurbation. In Victorian days and before competition from street tramways and buses the line enjoyed a fairly healthy passenger traffic, but once the local trams started it stood little chance, as the route described a complete semi-circle from Brighton station to Kemp Town and it became far quicker (and cheaper) to do the journey by road transport. Here we are looking approximately east towards the terminus from near Lewes Road station – for most of the line's history the only intermediate station on the branch – and the short siding adjacent to the station on the Kemp Town side may be seen in the foreground, together with its controlling ground frame and associated point rodding. Note the elaborately finished parapets of the viaduct – probably rarely appreciated by anyone but the local track gang. The single line continued to curve southwards before entering a 1,024 yard tunnel and arriving at Kemp Town station. Nothing now remains of the viaduct – being demolished in stages between 1976 and 1983. For those wondering, it was Cox's pill factory that was established in 1839 – although not at this location but the firm was clearly still going in 1952 – finally closing as Cox's Pharmaceuticals in 1979. Note also that magnificent weathercock on the right, surmounting the premises of Cox's factory. *RCR 4369.*

Opposite top: Turning to look in the other direction we see the decrepit remains of Lewes Road station and the buffers of the short siding. The station opened on 1st September 1873 – four years after the branch opened and, surprisingly, was provided with a platform on both sides of the running line. It closed to passengers with the cessation of passenger traffic on the branch on 1st January 1933 – the same day that the electrification of the main line into Brighton was inaugurated, so we can probably guess which event got the local publicity of the day. We are now looking approximately west towards the junction with the Brighton-Lewes line near the eastern portal of Ditchling Road tunnel. A coal yard of three sidings existed beyond the station building and remained open until the branch closed to goods traffic in 1971. For a time after closure to passengers the station became a pickle factory but the building was demolished in the mid-1950s leaving the platforms to await demolition in the 1970s. *RCR 4370.*

This page, bottom: Moving on to Kemp Town, we are now looking from the tunnel mouth southwards into the terminus – one mile and 32 chains from the junction with the Lewes line. The station building is centre background with the passenger platform immediately in front. During the early years of the 20th Century the branch was trialled with the LBSCR's steam railmotors, a couple of petrol railcars and pull-push trains. Only the latter proved a success but not sufficient to save the passenger service from an early demise and the usual train in later years was a "Terrier" tank and single "Balloon" auto trailer. Goods traffic continued until 26th June 1971 – coal to the right and general merchandise to the left – complete with yard crane. Note the interlaced four-way point at the station throat – essential to make maximum use of the site but probably a little inconvenient as all shunt moves had to enter the tunnel, situated immediately behind the photographer. Little railway evidence now remains – the site has become the Freshfield Industrial Estate and the tunnel mouth is used as a garage for road vehicles, being equipped with a roller shutter door. *RCR 4372.*

Two pictures of what look like a disused railway near Uckfield, East Sussex, seen on 27th August 1950. However, this track formation never even saw a train. In the early 1860s, the South Eastern and the newly formed London, Chatham & Dover Railways viewed the towns of Brighton and Eastbourne as likely destinations for their companies. The LBSCR saw this as a challenge to their monopoly and proposed a railway running south-eastwards from the southern end of Balcombe Viaduct on the Brighton main line, towards Lindfield, Uckfield and Hailsham, then re-joining the coast line somewhere near Bexhill and St. Leonards. Parliamentary authority was granted in 1864 but clearly the Brighton company was unconvinced that such a line would be profitable and construction proceeded only slowly. However, by starting work it ensured that the rival companies looked elsewhere for expansion. The financial crisis of 1866 and the collapse of banking firm Overend & Gurney – financier to much of the LBSCR – caused construction work to cease in February 1867, never to be resumed. By then some work had been done at the Balcombe Viaduct end as well as a start nearer Uckfield and a few relics of the line may be seen today. A look at Google Maps will also show small sections of the earthworks, although very little actual building work was ever completed. In the first picture a section of embankment approaching Uckfield may be seen, with the Uckfield line distant signal on the right (a line also now closed and dismantled) – this mound has now been removed and the field here is flat, while the second picture shows a partially completed occupation bridge a little further northwest. This still exists but is in parlous condition and completely surrounded by dense woodland. There were *Railway Magazine* articles about the line in the November/ December 1946 and September 1951 issues and no doubt the former brought the subject to Dick's notice – hence his August 1950 visit. Had the line been completed, the railway map of East Sussex would have looked very different and maybe Eastbourne, Bexhill and St. Leonards might have had a different – and perhaps more direct LBSCR route to London. Lindfield might also not have remained the picture-postcard village that it still is today, as a station would have been built at the northern end of the village. Alternatively, the whole thing could also have become another victim of Dr Beeching's axe.
RCR 4119 and 4120.

Opposite: Ex-LBSCR C2X 0-6-0 No. 32525 makes a rousing shunt into Knights Hill Sidings, Dulwich, on 5th May 1953. This was an ex-LNWR goods yard served off the LBSCR line between Peckham Rye and Tulse Hill – one of a number of "foreign" goods yards in the South London area – much needed when the domestic coal trade was at its height. It was shunted by a goods train that originated at Peckham Rye, hauled usually by a Brighton 0-6-0 of class C2 or C2X or an 0-6-2 tank of classes E3, E4, E5 or E6. After calling, the train ran on to Lillie Bridge sidings, handing empty wagons over to the LNWR and then picked up loaded traffic in the reverse direction, shunting Knights Hill yard again on the return journey to Peckham Rye. The two bridges (which span Rosendale Road) had most ornamental balustrades that were a requirement of any bridge built on land owned by Dulwich College. That on which the locomotive is shunting bore the date – 1891 – in fact the year before the yard opened. It comprised a fan of five sidings beyond the bridge that could accommodate 78 wagons and a run-round loop alongside the photographer, with entry/exit at each end – controlled from Knights Hill Sidings signal box, seen on the right. This was a standard Brighton box, of all-timber construction but note the ornamental metal ventilator-cum-finial on the top. On the main line alongside, an up train from Tulse Hill towards Peckham Rye is signalled, while in the background, above the left-hand bridge abutments, the wall surmounting Knights Hill Tunnel mouth may just be seen. Today, the yard has disappeared under residential development (Lairdale Close) and all that may be seen in Rosendale Road are new brick abutments where the yard bridge once crossed, while the 1868-vintage main line bridge has been renewed with a concrete-decked structure – but still retaining slightly ornamental metal balustrades. *RCR 4515.*

Above: Moving on to Peckham Rye, this is the old wagon hoist that transported coal wagons from rail level to the ground. Here the LBSCR is on a viaduct and at rail level there were just two loops – for incoming and outgoing traffic – each accommodating 20 wagons and these are just visible in the foreground. To reach ground level each wagon would be shunted on to a turntable and run into the cage to the left of the hoist using capstans and lowered to ground level where there were five more turntables and four roads equipped with capstans occupying the space between the two railway viaducts that could accommodate 73 wagons. The hoist was originally hydraulically-powered but since about 1925 had been powered by electricity. This is the scene on 10th October 1953 – a Saturday afternoon with by the look of it not very much going on. The depot was another "foreign" one – jointly operated by the LNWR and Midland Railways and opened in 1891. It only handled coal traffic and closed in 1958. To the end it was manned by a staff of three (foreman, capstan man and rope runner), all provided by the London Midland Region or its predecessors. The viaduct behind carries the ex-LCDR Catford Loop line and where repairs to the arches are in progress. Peckham Rye station is out of sight to the left. *RCR 4838.*

This page and opposite top: Two views of the ex-Midland Railway coal depot at Walworth Road – adjacent to the former LCDR line a quarter of a mile south of Elephant & Castle towards Loughborough Junction, opened as long ago as 1871. Unlike the coal depots at Knights Hill and Peckham Rye, Walworth Road was operated by a "foreign" locomotive - usually a condensing-apparatus fitted Jinty tank from Cricklewood hauling the trains (by 1954 just two daily) from Brent Yard. In fact, the traffic could have been satisfactorily dealt with by one trip, but there were restrictions on train length over the Metropolitan Widened Lines and the single reception road at Walworth could then only accommodate 23 wagons. This served 30 stub sidings accessible by a traverser, each capable of holding 2/3 wagons. A total of 113 coal chutes connected to ground level, so one can only imagine the surroundings being pretty dirty and dusty! These views date from 1st March 1957 and show the elevated signal box, the coal shed and ex-Midland Jinty 0-6-0 tank No. 47211. Ownership of the yard passed from the LM Region to the Southern on 1st May 1950 and by 1958 the timber structure showed signs of collapse, so the yard was closed for reconstruction in steel and concrete, reopening on 21st September 1959. In its final form it included both an arrival and departure road plus 50 unloading bays either side of a central traverser – each capable of accommodating a single wagon. This removed the previous problem whereby a wagon could be "trapped" on one of the stub roads by another in front of it. Thanks to this reconstruction, the depot lasted longer than most in the area, becoming part of the "House Coal Concentration" scheme of the 1960s and latterly served by 21-ton coal hopper wagons into the diesel era – possibly until at late as 2011. No trace of it now remains. (Note, the roof is cut-off on the original negative.) *RCR 8114 and 8114A.*

Although taken at Crystal Palace Low Level yard on 12th March 1954, this pre-Grouping era warning sign tells us that such procedures were commonplace in the days of steam at such locations as Knights Hill,

Peckham Rye and Walworth Road – amongst many, many others. Wagon doors made handy working platforms and could easily be opened to the horizontal position about 3-4 feet from the ground, propped using a couple of pieces of stout timber, and then used to shovel coal into sacks. It was all too easy, but the consequences of someone knocking out a prop were obvious. Nobody had heard of The Health and Safety at Work Act in 1954. *RCR 5053.*

PROPPING UP OF WAGON DOORS FOR SUPPORT OF COAL WEIGHING MACHINES OR FOR LOADING OR UNLOADING OF ANY DESCRIPTION OF TRAFFIC OR FOR ANY OTHER PURPOSE IS STRICTLY PROHIBITED. *BY ORDER OF L.B.& S.C.Ry.Cº*

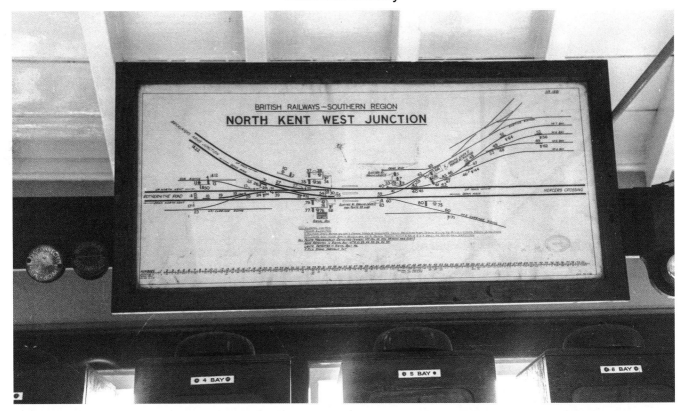

Above: An essential part of every signal box – the track diagram. This is the interior of North Kent West Junction box, photographed on 13th November 1954, situated near South Bermondsey station and controlling the approaches to Bricklayers Arms goods yard and locomotive sheds. As goods traffic faded, the box gradually declined in importance, finally closing in 1981, along with the Bricklayers Arms branch. It was an Evans O'Donnell structure dating from 1898 and once held an 80-lever frame. It retained its SECR name board "North Kent West Junction Signals" until closure. The location of the box is shown just left of lower centre of the layout, with the connecting line to the LBSCR at Bricklayers Arms Junction at top left, the line to the SECR North Kent routes lower left and right to Mercer's Crossing and further into Bricklayers Arms. No trace of the railway exists at this location today. *RCR 5642.*

Opposite page: Not very far away as the crow files, but requiring several reversals by rail, is the Deptford Wharf branch lift bridge and signal box. This ex-LBSCR line ran from New Cross Gate yards down to the River Thames at Deptford Wharf and was mainly used for coal and timber traffic until closure in 1964. There was also traffic to a Government Stores Depot in Grove Street, Deptford which necessitated the connecting spur running down a public road – something unlikely to be accepted today. The box was a very early design, timber on a brick base, dating from the 1850s and carried the simple title "Lift Bridge" with no indication of the wider location. Originally, the Deptford Wharf branch was authorised in 1846, for the LBSCR's predecessor, the London & Croydon Railway and opened in 1849 but on a slightly higher alignment rising to reach the LBSCR main line with a fixed bridge over the canal. Soon after the line was rerouted at lower level in order to go under the main line (seen crossing behind) and this required a lifting bridge across the Grand Surrey Canal. The canal company requested a swing bridge, but LBSCR objections overruled them and a hand-operated vertical lift bridge was provided instead. This was 13ft wide, 31ft 6in long and gave a headroom of 9ft 6in when raised. It was later electrically-operated but towards the end of its life the mechanism failed and a crane was employed to lift and lower the span on the few occasions when it needed to be raised. On 29th March 1958, E6 0-6-2 tank No. 32417 crosses the bridge with a short coal train bound for the wharf – the somewhat complicated mechanism may be seen, while the later picture shows the dismal scene looking south towards New Cross Gate yards on 14th November 1964 after lifting of the track and the removal of the bridge. Immediately beyond the bridge the divergence of tracks may be seen – left to the down side at New Cross Gate, right beneath the main line to the up side yard. The whole area remained semi-derelict for many years but has now been redeveloped and looks very different indeed – the canal now being a road. *RCR 11531 and 17749.*

Star Lane Intermediate signal box, on the LBSCR Quarry Line at Hooley, just south of Coulsdon. It opened in 1899 and was provided to increase line capacity by shortening the block section lengths. It also controlled two crossovers and a refuge siding and had a 15-lever frame. Of all-timber construction, it was situated in a deep cutting. Colour light signalling was provided over this section in 1932, as part of the full electrification to Brighton and many boxes were closed but Star Lane was retained for occasional use of the crossovers and the siding. For most of the time the box was unmanned and switched out, all signals being automatic. It was finally abolished on 22nd November 1978 after a long period of virtual disuse. This view dates from 23rd June 1956. RCR 7371

 A signal box at a very different location; this is the former Isle of Wight Central Railway box at Cowes, photographed on 25th June 1957. Cowes station was enlarged in 1892 and a 16-lever timber signal box provided by Saxby & Farmer. It was originally located at the end of the arrival platform - the latter several yards to the right. Further expansion of the station took place in 1918 and the box was moved to the location seen here, enlarged, mounted on a brick base and provided with a 22-lever frame. The original portion of the box is the three-window frame section on the right, the extension being that to the left of the green painted upright. The Saxby & Farmer cast plate may be seen below what would have been the original central window. The running - in board on the right is a standard Southern Railway concrete station name – manufactured at Exmouth Junction concrete works. The operation at Cowes was interesting to watch. After arrival, the locomotive would back the coaches a little out of the platform, run round using the crossover, after which the coaches would then be run downhill towards the buffer stops by gravity, under the control of the guard using the handbrake. The locomotive would then complete the run-round procedure, take water and reattach to the train for the return to Ryde Pier Head. It is believed occasional buffer stop impacts did occur, but none were serious. A procedure unlikely to be sanctioned nowadays! (Note, the roof is cut-off on the original negative.) *RCR 10833.*

Above: N class mogul No. 31865 comes up from Dunton Green towards Polhill tunnel and passes Polhill signal box on 25th June 1955, with a train from Dover or Folkestone to Charing Cross. The stock is of interest – a utility van leading special traffic set 211 in its 1955-58 formation comprising Bulleid/BRCW brake third 4226, Maunsell third 1906, Maunsell 'Restriction 1' former first, now third 658, "Thanet" composites 5527/26/24, "Thanet" third 989, Maunsell third 1131 and Bulleid/BRCW brake 4225 at the rear. Three of the "Thanets" are in crimson lake and cream – the rest of the train is malachite green. The signal box is a standard SECR timber structure on a stone base and remained in use until colour light signals replaced the semaphores – from 4th March 1962. Notice that the down signal is on the right-hand side of the line (complete with co-acting arm so it may be seen above or through the bridge on which Dick is standing), to be visible as trains came down the long left-hand curve towards Dunton Green station. It was not far south from here that "River" tank No. A800 and its train derailed at speed on 21st August 1927 resulting in the death of 13 passengers. As a result the entire class was withdrawn and rebuilt into 2-6-0 tender locomotives. *RCR 6156.*

Opposite: Most of the signal boxes between Clapham Junction and Waterloo were mounted above the tracks – once including Waterloo 'A' box located just outside the station. However, the latter, plus those further out to Vauxhall were replaced in 1936 by a single power box just outside the terminus, operating the colour light signals installed at that time. This is Loco Junction box, seen on 6th September 1958, just west of Queens Road Battersea and controls the exit from Nine Elms shed – out of sight on the right and from where the just visible Bulleid pacific is entering. The headcode indicates a light engine to Nine Elms shed and duty number 498 will probably be from Salisbury. Another Bulleid is visible in the distance beside one of the Nine Elms goods sheds. In the centre Urie S15 No. 30515 is heading down the line with either a local to Basingstoke or empty stock – it could be either as this was the last Saturday of the summer service. On the left an H15 waits by the entrance to Nine Elms goods yard and a 2-BIL electric heads up the local line towards Waterloo. *RCR 12715.*

We will now take a brief look at some Pullman Cars. Historically, the Pullman Car Company was responsible for all catering and catering vehicles on both the Central and South Eastern sections of the Southern – as a result of contracts signed many years before with the LBSCR and the SECR and from 1935 onwards the company staffed some SR-owned vehicles on these lines as well. The LSWR had instead opted to employ outside caterers but provided the dining cars themselves, so, apart from specific Pullman and boat trains most South Western section catering was provided using SR-built stock. All this gradually changed as the 1950s progressed, once the Pullman Car Company became a wholly-owned subsidiary of British Railways. Here Bulleid Q1 class 0-6-0 No. 33015 hauls the empty stock for the Bournemouth Belle away from Stewarts Lane towards Clapham Junction at 11am on 14th June 1959. On arrival there, another locomotive will be attached to the rear to take the stock up to Waterloo in time for departure for Bournemouth at 12.30pm. A similar repeat move in the reverse direction would take place in the early evening. This complicated series of empty stock workings were necessary because the Pullman Car Company had its London depot at Longhedge (Stewarts Lane) and it was not until February 1960 that the Belle stock was instead berthed at Clapham Junction sidings – being provisioned instead by road vehicles from the Battersea depot. Most of the Pullman cars in use at this time with the Belle were 12-wheelers and on this occasion the full 12-car load is being taken – weighing perhaps as much as 480 tons so quite a formidable load for the Merchant Navy pacific hauling the train. Rebuilt 1920-vintage brake parlour car No. 95 is the first vehicle, while the eighth and ninth are more modern eight-wheelers – usually only included in the train on Fridays and Saturdays, plus summer Sundays. Alongside, on Stewarts Lane shed is L1 class No. 31753. In the middle distance are a pair of ex-WR pannier tanks – perhaps en route to Folkestone Junction – although both Stewarts Lane and Nine Elms sheds had a small allocation of them around 1959-62. *RCR 13656.*

The next stage in the empty stock movement, seen on 26th July 1959. Urie H16 4-6-2 tank No. 30520 hauls the Bournemouth Belle stock away from Clapham Junction towards Waterloo platform 10, approaching Queens Road Battersea. This shows the other end of the rake, with brake car No. 41 leading – also dating from 1920 but this was built as a brake third car, unlike no. 95. This, and the next five cars are 12-wheelers, with an eight-wheeled car coming into shot on the left, so some remarshalling has taken place since the previous picture. The time is now likely to be around midday. The Bournemouth Belle was introduced on Sunday 5th July 1931, initially running at weekends only until January 1936 when it became a daily service, with a down departure time of 10.30am. For the first summer Poole, Wareham, Dorchester and Weymouth were also served but this was not perpetuated. Like almost all other Pullman services, the train was suspended during World War 2 and recommenced, daily, from 7th October 1946 but retimed to leave Waterloo at 12.30pm. The final run was on the last day of Southern steam, 9th July 1967, but despite the machinations of a number of railwaymen, the last trip was not behind steam but a Brush type 4 diesel locomotive. By this time the Pullmans were all more modern eight-wheelers topped and tailed by a BR Mk 1 full brake – the latter either green or corporate image blue and grey. For a time in the early 1960s, the Southern Region employed a pair of Western Region chocolate and cream vans, numbers W80713/14 and these matched the Pullman cars very much better. *RCR 13965.*

At Eardley Road sidings on 18th April 1960 is 12-wheeled first class Pullman *Palmyra*. This was built by Birmingham Railway Carriage & Wagon Company in January 1921 for service on the SECR. It was a kitchen car (this is behind the shallow windows at the left-hand end) with 16 first class seats. It measured 63ft 6in long and was allocated to Pullman Car Diagram 25K. It spent almost its whole life on the South Eastern section – running both in boat trains or singly providing catering facilities in trains otherwise composed of SR stock. This was the norm on both the South Eastern and the Central sections of the Southern – Pullman provided the staff, the food and the beverages – and made the profit! They did this even if the catering vehicle was Southern-owned so small wonder they complained when Bullied built his "Bognor Buffet" cars with their "art-deco" interiors in 1938. Passengers lingered long over a cup of coffee and turnover suffered. Bulleid's post-war answer was his windowless Tavern cars and accompanying diners – guaranteed to make passengers bolt their meal and return to their seats in the rest of the train – to continue enjoying the passing scenery! Pullman *Palmyra* retained full bodyside panelling and matchboarding below the waistline until withdrawal in October 1960, unlike some cars that became aluminium-sheeted in an attempt to make them look more modern. However, the car got a further lease of life by being sold to the Eastern Region, becoming their blue-liveried camping coach CC168, serving for a few more years in either a Norfolk or Suffolk coastal location until 1967. *RCR 14667.*

Eight-wheeled K class Pullman *Isle of Thanet* outside the carriage shed at Longhedge (Stewarts Lane) on 15th September 1957, roofboarded for an Ocean Liner Express to Southampton Docks. This car had a most interesting and varied history. It was built in October 1925 for CIWL service in Italy, reaching there via the Harwich-Zeebrugge train ferry and carried the name *Leona* and number CIWL 53. It was part of a group of 10 Pullmans shipped abroad at that time. Two subsequently went to Egypt, the other eight returned to Britain in late 1929. Refurbished by Midland RCW Co., it was renamed *Princess Elizabeth*, entering SR service as a parlour first with 24 seats – to Pullman Diagram 105P – being noted on the Golden Arrow in the early 1930s and Southampton Docks boat trains by 1938. At some time a handbrake was fitted (at the end nearest the camera - note the word 'Guard' discernable on the open door) and it was then rediagrammed 105B. In November 1950 it was renamed *Isle of Thanet*, soon after being refurbished yet again for use on the Golden Arrow. This refurbishment included the fitting of rectangular, instead of oval, toilet windows while the guard's compartment was enlarged slightly. Note that the nearest door is not a passenger-access door and leads to the brake/luggage compartment. The original matchboarding and panelling was plated over at the same time. The coach achieved fame on 30th January 1965 when included in Sir Winston Churchill's funeral train from Waterloo to Handborough, Oxfordshire. Withdrawn in August 1967, the car accompanied *Flying Scotsman* to America in 1969. When bankruptcy loomed for Alan Pegler, *Isle of Thanet* was sold into preservation in the USA, finally returning to Britain in 2002 along with the hearse van from Sir Winston's funeral train. It currently resides at Carnforth. The Italianate style building behind is part of the former LCDR Longhedge Works buildings – the originals were all built in this very distinctive style. *RCR 11215.*

Two Pullman cars from a much earlier era, both grounded at the then new Preston Park Works in 1931/32 for use as canteen facilities and stores respectively, seen on 6th June 1951. The first picture shows former first class car *Devonshire*, built in 1900 in the USA for service on the LBSCR. It would have been brought to this country as a kit of parts and assembled at Brighton. This was a kitchen car and measured 64ft long and 8ft 9in wide, complete with clerestory roof. It originally had 32 seats – later reduced to 28. It ran on six-wheeled all-timber bogies – of the type seen under *Palmyra* in a previous picture. The car was normally used on the "Brighton Limited" – a forerunner of the Southern Belle/Brighton Belle. The second picture shows an even older car – *Albert Edward* of 1877 vintage. This was built by Pullman at their Detroit works in America and shipped to Britain for re-assembly at Derby Works of the Midland Railway. It was also a kitchen car, 58ft long and 8ft 9in wide and ran on eight-wheeled bogies, with seats for 34 first class passengers. It was sent to the LBSCR in October 1877, where it remained for the rest of its life. In 1915 it was demoted to third class car No. 4, whose length was also recorded as 59ft 3in, not 58ft! However, this could possibly be explained by the fact that the car as built had American-style open ended balconies – these were later enclosed. In this form it seated 56 passengers, together with a somewhat smaller kitchen area. Third class Pullmans were a rare phenomenon in 1915 and, unlike ordinary carriage stock, have always been in the minority. Notice that, because of their "monocoque" construction, the cars retained their truss rodding even when grounded. Preston Park works closed in November 1963 and the building lay semi-derelict for some time, more recently being used to store various railway artefacts intended for preservation. Vandalism inevitably struck – despite the difficulty of accessing the site as it was hemmed in by railways on all sides, and the stock was cleared during 2008, with demolition following soon after. *RCR 4238 and 4239.*

Living in Tulse Hill, Dick would see Southern Electric trains daily and his camera duly recorded them as well. We will now look at a number of these – and they are not nearly as monotonous as many would believe! 2-SL electric unit 1806 passes Peckham Rye 'C' signal box and enters the station on 7th March 1953, with a train from London Bridge to Victoria – headcode 2. The South London line was the first LBSCR line to be electrified on the 6700V AC overhead system, full electric services commencing on 1st December 1909 and the system was further extended into the suburbs in the ensuing years. The electrical equipment came from Germany but not surprisingly World War 1 halted development and the last scheme was not energised until early post-Grouping days. Despite the technical superiority of the LBSCR system, the Southern Railway found itself with a greater mileage of the ex-LSWR's 3rd rail DC electrification – this was also far cheaper to install – so it was perhaps inevitable that the Brighton AC system was doomed from the start. Conversion of the South London line to DC operation was completed in June 1928. For this, some of the former LBSCR South London AC stock was converted into 2-car units 1901-8 (later 1801-8) and these ran the service until withdrawn in 1954, assisted occasionally by the similar 2-WIM units 1809-12. Peckham Rye 'C' was a typically attractive Brighton timber signal box, controlling the entry to the goods yard and wagon hoist – just seen to the left of the electric unit and described in a previous picture - see page 71. The signal marked 'S' controlled the "shunt ahead" move towards the next signal, allowing the goods train to then reverse into the yard – there being no facing entry into the two sidings at this end. (Again the top of the signal does not appear on the negative.) *RCR 4430.*

Left: Replacement electric stock for the South London line came in the form of 2-EPB units numbered from 5701 upwards in 1954. Almost new BR unit No. 5701 stands at Queens Road, Peckham while working the 1.48pm London-Bridge to Victoria service on 4th March 1954 – probably an early trial run as the ex-Brighton AC units could still be seen on the line until September of that year. These new units were intended, not just for the South London line but also the Wimbledon-West Croydon service and also for the Eastern section "10-car scheme" – a total of 79 units being delivered between late 1953 and 1958. A further unit, No. 5800, was added in 1960 (a replacement for unit 5766, destroyed at St Johns on 4th December 1957) while the 15 slightly different ex-Tyneside electric units became Southern Region stock in 1964, numbered 5781-95 and these could also be seen on the South London and Wimbledon-West Croydon services. *RCR 5037.*

Bottom: The other place to see these units could hardly have been more different. The South London line ran mostly on viaducts and embankments above suburbia – the Wimbledon-West Croydon line was partially single-track and ran through suburbia, countryside and through the National Trust's Morden Hall Park and industrial scenery around Waddon Marsh towards West Croydon, complete with gated level crossings. The only similarities came with the stock and the route headcode – 2 again. Until September 1954 the line was the province of the 2-WIM ex-AC units (assisted by the occasional 2-SL unit), after which the BR 2-EPB's took over. On 13th March 1955, unit 5716 leaves Merton Park towards Mitcham Junction and West Croydon. On the right, the platforms serving the line to Merton Abbey (and once through to Tooting Junction) may be seen – goods only from March 1929 until closure of that section in May 1975. For a number of years this goods siding served the Lines Brothers *Triang* factory at Merton Abbey and would see their distinctive dark blue containers on BR conflat wagons from the early 1960s. Note that the ex-LBSCR station name is still visible – only partially obscured by a BR green enamel sign. The West Croydon line platform continued to see BR trains until 31st May 1997, when it was closed and converted into part of the Croydon Tramlink system. *RCR 5683.*

Right: Ex-LSWR 4-SUB unit, No. 4245 emerging from the northern portal of the 331 yard long Knights Hill Tunnel on 5th May 1953, with a Crystal Palace Low Level to London Bridge service. In fact, this train would have started from London Bridge and reached Crystal Palace via Forest Hill – one of a number of Central section circular services. The northern portal was fairly ornamented, but the southern portal, visible from Tulse Hill station, was even more ornate. The electric unit was converted from LSWR bogie "block"

coach bodies on new underframes in May/June 1928, becoming 3-car unit 1687 (coach numbers 8208, 9336, 8822). In October 1948, ex-LSWR trailer coach 9216 was added and the unit became 4-SUB 4245 until withdrawn in April 1954. *RCR 4519.*

Bottom: Another ex-LSWR 4-SUB unit, No. 4204 passes the disused Clapham Cutting signal box in May 1953, heading for Dorking North. This LSWR type 2 box was erected about 1885 and ceased to function as a signal box when the Waterloo colour light signalling and Wimbledon flyover came into use in 1936, altering the pairing of tracks over this section from up local, up fast, down fast, down local to up fast, down fast, up local, down local. This train is therefore on the down local line – the only one not changed. Unit 4204 has an interesting history. Converted in August 1915 from LSWR bogie "block" stock, it became LSWR electric unit E41. This was renumbered as SR unit 1241 after the Grouping but retained its original South Western "torpedo" front end and short 51ft underframes. SR coach numbers were 8061, 9424 and 8062. In December 1937 the unit was taken out of service and the bodies remounted on new SR standard 62ft underframes – two new compartments being added to the original bodywork of each vehicle. It returned to traffic, carrying the same unit and coach numbers, only to be augmented to a 4-SUB unit in May 1944 by the addition of another lengthened LSWR coach previously formed in a 2-coach trailer unit, No. 9247 (the third coach in the picture) and renumbered as unit 4204. In this form it continued in traffic until November 1955. This was not the end, however, as all four underframes were reused for 4-EPB coaches and they remained in service until 1991-93. Not a bad record for recycling! *RCR 3538.*

Above: Ex-LBSCR 4-SUB unit No. 4548 at Tulse Hill on a London Bridge to London Bridge via Tulse Hill, Selhurst and Forest Hill service on 27th May 1956 – as indicated by the V+ two dots over headcode. Why on earth a simple numbering system was not employed from the outset cannot be fathomed, but it was complicated enough for railwaymen to follow, never mind the travelling public! In the end, resort was made to upside down letters, back-to-front letters, one dot, two dots or a bar over the letters, to try to distinguish individual routes. It would have been so much simpler with numbers, but that took a new generation of electric units before it was adopted on the suburban routes. Perhaps it all added to the charm! Unit 4548 started electric stock life in January 1930 as 3-car unit 1751, converted from LBSCR steam stock on new 62ft underframes – coach numbers being 8720, 9462 and 8886. In May 1949 a Bulleid 10-compartment all-steel trailer coach was added (No. 10188) and the unit renumbered as 4548. Presumably accident damage occurred a year later as the formation then changed to 8700, Bulleid coach 10469 (the second coach in the picture), 9462, 8886. Two of the three ex-LBSCR coaches were withdrawn in October 1956, leaving coach 9462 to run in "new" unit 4515 until November 1959, while the Bulleid coach became 4-EPB trailer 15064 in unit 5246 until March 1975. *RCR 7285.*

Opposite top: For once this headcode shows some logic! 1925-vintage 4-SUB unit No. 4311 heads for Hampton Court, between Queens Road and Clapham Junction on 26th July 1959. The original ex-LSWR letter codes of 1915 were, for the most part, meaningful, as follows: - H was for Hampton Court, P for Wimbledon via East Putney, S for Shepperton, O for 'Ounslow (!) and V for the Kingston roundabout route – i.e. Thames Valley. The only exception was I – which applied to the short-lived Claygate via Surbiton service, although some logic was applied later when the letter was used for a Woking via Brentford, Isleworth and Camberley route. A certain bread manufacturer soon spotted the fact that the letters spelt out their famous product and soon every compartment displayed an advert for HOVIS – "The route to good health has HOVIS at the end" with five electric trains showing the appropriate headcodes. Was this by accident or design?? Unit 4311 was built new in June 1925 – one of 26 3-car units for the South Western section electrification to Guildford and Dorking. Originally numbered 1296, it was formed of motor brake thirds 8149/50 (built by Metropolitan) and trailer composite 9446 (built by BRCW). These 26 units were the last built to the LSWR specification with "torpedo" driving cabs, designed by the ex-LSWR

electrical engineer, Herbert Jones. In December 1945 a Bulleid 10-compartment trailer was added, number 10379; the third coach visible and as 4-SUB unit 4311, it remained in traffic until April 1961. The unit was broken up at Newhaven during 1963. *RCR 13954.*

Bottom: The old and the new together outside Peckham Rye maintenance workshops on 28th February 1957. Kent Coast 4-CEP motor brake second S61039 is undergoing tests and stands alongside ex-LBSCR motor brake composite S8889S of unit 4511 – one of 18 ex-Brighton 4-SUB units retained and reformed as an interim measure during 1956-59 – and destined to be the last all-timber bodied rebuilt suburban electric units in service. As may be seen, the old and new are not compatible – either in electrical equipment or couplings – one has traditional screw couplings, the other buckeye automatic. The line on the left is towards Tulse Hill, that on the right towards Victoria. Nothing of the workshops remain today – the site being given over to residential development but Peckham Rye station remains an important interchange. *RCR 10244.*

Opposite top: A number of the Kent Coast electric units were stored for a short time between Ardingly and Horsted Keynes before entering traffic. On 17th May 1959 unit 7128 heads a long line of units awaiting the switch-on of phase 1 of the Kent Coast electrification, which took place just a month later on 15th June 1959. They are standing on

the former down line. In those days, such a location in open country could be regarded as reasonably vandal free – although the up line was still being used for the hourly electric service from Horsted Keynes to Seaford, so railway staff were at least present to keep an eye on matters for some of the time. The location was also later used to store ex-steam stock awaiting breaking up at Newhaven and in December 1961 no less than 144 (mostly withdrawn) coaches were noted standing on the branch. *RCR 7865.*

Opposite bottom: A main line unit from an earlier generation, this is 6-PUL unit 3006 approaching Star Lane signal box on the Quarry line on 23rd June 1956, while working a non-stop Victoria-Brighton service. As was usual at this time, the second unit is a 6-PAN. The motor coaches from these Brighton-line 6-car units were "all-motored", tipping the scales at 59 tons and, at 75 miles per hour, were soon found to punish the track fairly severely. A ride in the motor coach was always pretty lively and this became worse as the units approached the ends of their lives in the mid-1960s. For enthusiasts it just added to the fun, but it should be noted that the far newer Kent Coast units also soon became well-known for their rough riding. Your writer occasionally commuted from Waterloo East to Ashford during the early 1970s and tried to ensure he travelled in a 4-CEP running on "Commonwealth" bogies whenever possible, otherwise writing whilst belting along the Tonbridge-Ashford straight at 90mph was well-nigh impossible! *RCR 7372.*

Above: Another perennial problem with the third rail electric system was, of course, ice. In order to combat this a number of coaches were converted to de-icing cars, capable of spraying de-icing fluid on to the conductor rails during overnight shutdown. These took two forms – either 2-car powered units or trailer coaches capable of being inserted between ordinary units in scheduled de-icing trains or being loco-hauled around the system. The writer can only recall a couple of occasions when one was actually inserted in a passenger-carrying service – this being during a winter rail strike in the early 1980s. The first generation of the trailer cars were former LBSCR 9-compartment thirds but the second batch were ex-4-SUB trailer cars such as DS70087, seen in company with DS70086 at Peckham Rye depot on Boxing Day 1960. This was former 10-compartment third 10400 from 4-SUB unit No. 4349, converted earlier in 1960 – one of four such conversions at that time. Although not obvious from the picture, the livery was departmental red but all four lasted long enough to carry rail blue livery. This coach was the last in use, and renumbered as ADB977364 it lasted to 2010, later carrying Network South East "toothpaste stripe" livery and finally a two-tone sand colour finish. It was then sold into private preservation in Oxfordshire but is believed to be again for sale. *RCR 15525.*

Opposite: Slade Green depot, near Dartford – where many of the South Eastern section suburban units are based – seen on 8th November 1958. This began life as a steam shed in 1901, originally called Slades Green and was a huge eight-road building with two more repair bays at one end. Outside were two 50ft turntables – one at each end of the yard. Designed to cater for 110 locomotives, the allocation was mainly small suburban tanks. With the completion of the first stage of the South Eastern suburban electrification in 1926, the building was converted to house electric multiple units and has remained in use ever since - with a major reconstruction in 1990/91. Visible here are several 4-SUB units and their 1951 development; the 4-EPB units, including 4696, 5019 and 5198, while 2-EPB unit 5712 is just seen on the right. These had all passed into history by 1995 and the reconstructed depot today houses more modern EMUs.
RCR 12972.

Above: Bulleid 4 SUB unit No. 4676 stands at the semi-derelict former LCDR terminus at Crystal Palace High Level on 19th July 1954, having arrived with a train from Blackfriars. By now just a single 4-car unit sufficed. This was the second station built to serve the re-sited Great Exhibition building at Crystal Palace, opening on 1st August 1865 and was served by a branch that left the Victoria-Dartford-Gravesend line at Nunhead. Electrified in July 1925, traffic remained at just about acceptable levels until the Crystal Palace burnt down in 1936, after which decline set in – all too apparent in the picture, with ferns growing out of parts of the structure. The branch was closed for periods of both world wars, being used for stock storage and complete closure took place on 20th September 1954. Much of the building remained derelict until 1961. The site is now a housing estate with just one retaining wall and the tunnel mouth outside the station remaining visible. Some other parts of the station access subways remain but may only be visited on specific heritage open days. *RCR 5193.*

Chapter 10

(A few) Branch Lines

This page: The final train to serve Crystal Palace High Level, on 19th September 1954. This is the empty stock of the "*Palace Centenarian*", hauled by C class 0-6-0 No. 31719 (just seen with chimney coupled to the train) and sister engine No. 31576. The locomotives are about to uncouple to use the turntable beyond the station and return to the other end of the train. The second picture shows No. 31576 being turned. The train departed at about 2.20pm and made a circular journey around London, including Brixton, Clapham Junction, Barnes, Richmond, around the Kingston loop back to Wimbledon, East Putney, Clapham Junction, Herne Hill, Crystal Palace Low Level, Forest Hill, New Cross Gate, London Bridge and into Blackfriars. After reversal there the train returned to Crystal Palace High Level via Peckham Rye and Nunhead, arriving around 7pm. For most of the journey, only loco 31576 was used so possibly No. 31719 only assisted on the climb to the high level station. This was almost certainly the only time the station saw a buffet car. All coaches visible are of Maunsell design (8-set 430 plus buffet car) and at least three of them are corridor firsts. The tour was privately organised and the fare was 6/- (30 pence – a bargain!!). *RCR 5517 and 5519.*

Opposite top: Another line that climbed was the ex-SER branch from Paddock Wood to Hawkhurst – although in reality that town was not well-served by the terminus, as it was situated a good mile or more to the north in a rather elevated position. There were plans to extend the line to Tenterden and Rye but these never materialised, hence the layout was built to allow easy conversion into a through station. H class tank No. 31543 is at the end of the line on 20th May 1961, hauling a Maunsell pull-push set. The branch opened throughout on 4th September 1893, closing just three weeks after Dick's visit – on 12th June 1961.

Despite through coaches to London at various stages in the line's history, passenger traffic was always light. In its final days the branch was used for filming a children's TV programme – "*The Old Pull 'n Push*" – broadcast by ITV in 1960/61. The site is now a business park and, remarkably, the signal box, engine and goods shed all survive in good condition. The station has also been reproduced in model form a number of times. *RCR 15774.*

Bottom: Opportunities to examine various cost-cutting procedures on branch lines seem to have seldom been taken during the 1950s – storing up problems in the following decade only to be drastically solved by Dr Beeching's axe. One

experiment that was tried was the use of this ACV lightweight diesel railbus on the Hundred of Hoo branch in 1953. The original three-car unit is seen at Cliffe, en route to Allhallows, on 24th October, alongside the more traditional branch line train, hauled by a C class 0-6-0. These cars were nicknamed "the flying bricks" and were tried in many places but most successfully on several LMR branches, including St Albans-Watford and Harrow- Belmont lines – all being based at Watford Junction. The LMR eventually purchased eleven such vehicles (and they were allocated BR running numbers) but they were not judged a success and all were broken up in 1963; none having been used since 1960. The underframes were built by AEC, the bodies by Park Royal. The livery of the original trio was two-tone grey with red lining and buffer beams – later vehicles were BR green. The Allhallows branch seems to have been their only use on the Southern Region whilst at least one trial also took place on the WR. An opportunity missed, perhaps? *RCR 4850.*

Above: The ex-LSWR mid-Hants route from Alton to Winchester was always referred to by enginemen as "going over the Alps" since at Medstead the line reached the highest point on the Southern Railway in the south-east – 652 feet above sea level. The LSWR arrived at Alton from Guildford in 1852, extending through Medstead, Ropley and Alresford to re-join the main line north of Winchester in 1865. The line was regularly used as a diversionary route during engineering works and the 8th May 1955 (a Sunday) was one such occasion. Here the 3.35pm Waterloo-Bournemouth breasts the summit behind Lord Nelson class 4-6-0 No. 30858 *Lord Duncan*. This scene could almost be replicated today, since the present day "Watercress Line" operates over the route and is now home to the NRM's *Lord Nelson* – although currently the locomotive has been withdrawn from service and now awaits an overhaul. *RCR 6059.*

Opposite top: A little later in the day, a Waterloo-Weymouth 12-coach troop special heads away from Alton towards Medstead behind West Country pacific No. 34012 *Launceston*, assisted by 700 class goods No. 30700. The stock is mostly Maunsells, with two Bulleid coaches on the rear. On days such as this, even the Bournemouth Belle would travel via Alton, leaving the main line at Pirbright Junction and re-joining it at Winchester Junction. During the run up to the Bournemouth line electrification in 1965-66, this was a common weekend occurrence but ceased on electrification, simply because the line beyond Alton

was not electrified and closed on 5th February 1973. Reopened in stages since 1977, the preserved watercress line is now a major tourist attraction in the area. *RCR 6064.*

Opposite bottom: The more usual branch line train between Winchester and Alton – M7 0-4-4 tank No. 30480 propels pull-push set 31 out of Medstead & Four Marks station towards Alton on Sunday 8th May 1955. It had just waited for Merchant Navy No. 35019 to pass on a down Bournemouth service so was probably running late. Pull-push set 31 is formed of ex-SECR brake third No. 3474 and ex-LSWR 58ft rebuilt composite No. 4730. For the final 15 years of the BR service on the mid-Hants route, trains were formed of 2/3-car Hampshire diesel units. The signal box seen in the picture was closed on 23rd January 1967 and later demolished. The present box at this location comes from Wilton and became operational in October 1985 but is almost identical to the original. *RCR 6062.*

Opposite page: A1X class No. 32678 collects old wagons from the west quay branch at Newhaven Harbour, just prior to closure, on a rather wet 27th July 1963. This branch left the main line at the back of Newhaven goods yard and crossed the swing bridge before turning to run down the west side of the River Ouse, serving several warehouses, landing stages and a quarry before running out on to the west breakwater. By the 1960s there was little traffic over the line and most of the wagons seen here were "internal users" – for use only at the harbour and were not permitted to run on the main line – note that they are all marked with a large cross to indicate this fact. The second picture shows other wagons being collected; in this case a former GWR van and a Southern gangwayed bogie luggage van – either internal user No. 081153 or 081154 – previously Nos. 2360 and 2366 respectively which were used as a stores vans there from December 1959 onwards. The branch finally closed during August 1963. For very many years it was always shunted by a "Terrier" tank and two were usually sub-shedded at Newhaven for the purpose. The departure of No. 32678 from Newhaven on 18th August marked the end of a 65-year association between the class and the Newhaven Harbour Company and its successors. No. 32678 survives today on the Kent & East Sussex Railway. *RCR 17291 et seq.*

Above: LBSCR E4 0-6-2 tank No. 32504 departs from West Hoathly towards Lewes on 13th March 1958, hauling a solitary LBSCR pull-push driving brake coach – probably No. 3847 – as this was allocated to the line at the time. The Lewes-East Grinstead line was closed by BR on 13th June 1955 – although due to the prolonged ASLEF rail strike the final train actually ran on 28th May. Local resident Madge Bessemer unearthed a clause in the original act for the railway compelling the service to run for not less than 999 years unless prior notice was given and campaigned successfully for a reinstatement. This was done grudgingly by BR from 7th August 1956 but with the minimum statutory service of just four trains a day – often at inconvenient times – hence it became known as "the sulky service". BR duly took steps to repeal the original railway act and the line closed for a second time on 17th March 1958 – just a few days after Dick's final visit. All this brought the line to the notice of the general public and allowed the present-day Bluebell Railway preservationists to marshal their forces and be ready to commence operation of the line between Sheffield Park and Horsted Keynes on August bank holiday 1960. Dick was an enthusiastic supporter of the preservation group and acted as consulting editor for their magazine 'Bluebell News' for over ten years until the spring of 1971. *RCR 11498.*

We will now continue with some more rolling stock pictures, finally ending with goods vehicles.

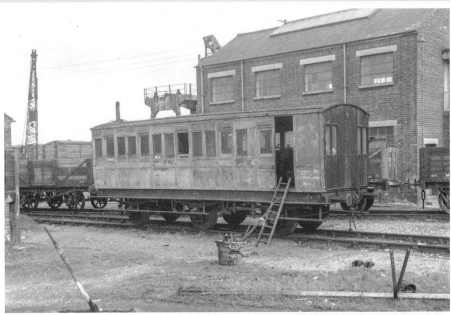

This page, top: The last ex-LCDR coach on the mainland on BR was this former brake third; departmental No. 873s, seen at Redbridge sleeper works on 23rd May 1953. Built in October 1894 as a 30ft four-compartment brake, LCDR No. 48, it became SECR No. 2781 after 1899 and SR No. 3630 after 1923, allocated to SR Diagram 173. It ran at one end of set 837 – a 14-coach formation stabled at Crystal Palace and was used on excursion and special traffic duties to the coast – probably only on high days and holidays. Withdrawn from these duties in 1935, it was converted into departmental coach 873s and allocated to Redbridge, where it saw out its BR days. Withdrawn again in 1949, it was reinstated and lasted finally until August 1961. It was then purchased by the Bluebell Railway, arriving there in February 1962. Apart from a quick external repaint in green, no further restoration has taken place and the coach is currently used as a store for the carriage & wagon department. *RCR 4604.*

This page, bottom: A rake of ten former SNCF mineral wagons parked on the Rye Harbour branch on 21st September 1950. These vehicles had all been shipped to France following D-Day to assist in the Allied push towards Berlin and the refurbishment of the French railway system and many of them were returned to Britain from 1949 onwards, being stripped of their foreign fittings and made ready for British Railways service. At that time BR was desperately short of serviceable goods stock – especially mineral wagons – so this proved very timely. All bar one of those visible are Charles Roberts design "slope-sided" minerals that had been built by various contractors from 1939 onwards and to Ministry of War Transport orders between 1944 and 1947. Very many were subsequently taken into BR stock and allocated BR Diagram 1/100. The Rye Harbour branch had often been used to store wagons awaiting entry to Ashford Works. *RCR 4193.*

Opposite: The melancholy scene at West Hoathly on 23rd May 1964, just before demolition began. This is looking south, with the 731 yard long Sharpthorne Tunnel in the background. By August, demolition was in full swing, assisted by the Bluebell's North London tank locomotive No. 27257. Eventually, almost all trace of the station was removed and although the Bluebell Railway now runs through the station site there are no definite plans to rebuild a station here. *RCR 17626.*

Opposite top: An ex-LBSCR covered goods wagon transferred to the Isle of Wight, at Ryde St. Johns on 25th June 1957. No. DS46957 was a fully Westinghouse-braked example of SR Diagram 1436 and dates from 1922 as LBSCR No. 3649 and one of the last vans built by the company before the Grouping. Renumbered as SR mainland 46762, it was shipped to the Isle of Wight in February 1929, to be renumbered again. It entered departmental stock in March 1954, receiving the letter 'D' in front of its Southern Region number. The livery is SR brown with white lettering on black patches. As a departmental tool van, it moved infrequently around the Island network until withdrawal on 12th October 1968. Similar vans are preserved both on the Isle of Wight and at the Bluebell Railway. *RCR 10840.*

Opposite bottom: An ex-LSWR 24ft passenger luggage van in departmental use at Edenbridge Town yard on 4th June 1955. No. DS1624 carries a rather intriguing inscription "Show Traffic Equipment. Return to Horsham SR". However, to what this refers is unknown - a circus perhaps? The van actually dates from December 1923, but built to an LSWR design that goes back to 1909 and carried SR traffic number 1630, allocated to Diagram 929. Withdrawn in August 1941, it entered departmental use as No. 1624s until July 1945 – likely for some wartime purpose. It was then returned to traffic stock as No. 1630, but more probably languished in a siding somewhere until returned to departmental stock in May 1953 – especially since the number 1630 had been reissued to a new "utility van" by that time! It was then relettered as shown and finally condemned in May 1959. The additional "tin" roof has probably been provided for one of two reasons – either as extra heat insulation or because the original roof was leaking! *RCR 6142.*

Above: Southern Railway ferry van No. 3 at Eardley Road sidings on 18th April 1960 – flanked by Nos. 1 and 2. These had been built in June 1936 for the Night Ferry service – hence the inclusion of the central "birdcage" lookout to satisfy European railway regulations. They were also painted Wagon-Lits blue to match the sleeping cars forming the rest of the train. These vans were 36ft long and to SR Diagram 3091. All three no longer conformed to Continental requirements from early 1960 and were replaced on the Night Ferry by Continental baggage vans. Here they await stripping of Westinghouse brakes and repainting into ordinary green livery, which took place in October 1960, after which they were used turn and turn about with the standard BY passenger brake vans until withdrawn between 1969 and 1974. No. 3 was the final survivor, taken out of traffic in July 1974. *RCR 14670.*

Opposite: BR Continental ferry van No. B889001 at Rotherhithe Road carriage sidings on 31st July 1958 – when almost brand new and clearly in a line of similar vehicles. Thirty of these four-wheelers (plus four bogie vans of 1955) were built for Dover-Dunkirk ferry traffic between 1958 and 1961, numbered as goods wagons and finished in fitted freight stock bauxite livery. They were 30ft 9in long and resembled the prototype BR general utility van E94100 in appearance. Later, they had their windows plated over which altered their appearance considerably. Despite being classed as goods wagons, they ran regularly as tail traffic in passenger trains on the South Eastern section. BR Diagram 291 was allocated and some ran until the 1980s. *RCR 12533.*

Above: As the last vehicle in a goods train, appropriately we will conclude this section with a look at some brake vans. This is a former SECR six-wheeled 20-tonner to SR Diagram 1558 at Redbridge on 23rd May 1953 – one of a class of 90 such vehicles. Built in June 1909 as SECR No. 2040, it originally had one open and one closed balcony – almost a carbon copy of similar vans built for the Midland Railway. Between 1914 and 1920 the open balconies were enclosed – giving the vans a more balanced – and modern appearance. Renumbered as SR 55394 after the Grouping, the van would have been used on South Eastern section main line goods trains until January 1950, when it was one of four transferred to departmental stock and given the 'DS' prefix, and through vacuum piped for use with long-welded rail trains. Diagram 1913 was then allocated to these four vans and they were some of the last of the type to survive, sometime after 1960. Just one remains in existence today – on the Kent & East Sussex Railway. *RCR 4606.*

Top: At Brockenhurst on 8th September 1953 is ex-LSWR ballast brake van DS61922. This was one of 26 such vans built between 1898 and 1911, formerly LSWR Engineer's department No. 11. Now painted in BR ED black with yellow lettering, it was rated at 10 tons tare (actually a little heavier) but three of the vans were uprated to 15 tons in early Southern Railway days. They were 18ft long, with a wheelbase of 10ft 6in. SR Diagram 1736 was allocated. The last survivor was No. 61931, which could still be seen at Eastleigh P. Way depot in mid-1966. Despite being a ballast brake, it is parked in a line of mineral wagons, so maybe the "no brake" chalked inscription meant it was heading for repair somewhere. There was a small wagon repair facility in Brockenhurst yard. *RCR 4793.*

Right: An ex-LSWR brake van, also at Brockenhurst but on 24th May 1953. This is Diagram 1542 17-ton van No. S54946 – although the official tare rating was 18 tons – and was boarded to work between Brockenhurst and Lymington only. This was its final duty and it performed this function over the years 1948 until withdrawal in 1954. To the end the livery remained SR brown with red ends. There were just four of these vans, dating from 1906 and the original drawing shows six wheels but whether they were built as such is not known. If they were, then it was not long before they were reduced to four wheels, so perhaps braking power was found wanting and better results were achieved as a 4-wheeler. Until 1906, ex-LSWR brake vans were small 10-tonners – built on the same underframe as the ballast brake in the previous picture, but after this date heavier vans were found to be necessary, as seen overleaf. *RCR 4610.*

'Southern Medley'

Opposite top: Also at Brockenhurst on 24th May 1953 is a Diagram 1543 20-ton van, No. S55032, in BR grey with black number patches. Its LSWR number was 4699. A total of 75 such vans were built between 1915 and 1921, with a further 25 rather similar (but wider) vans to Diagram 1547, completed in 1922/23. Always known to the goods guards as "new" vans – even thirty years later – they could be found on many South Western section main line goods trains until the late 1950s – some appearing on the Central and South Eastern sections later, although they were not allowed on the Tonbridge-Hastings line, as noted on the side board . A few remained in service until 1962/63. Most were built as 20-tonners, but many were later uprated to 24 or 25 tons tare. *RCR 4611.*

Opposite bottom: A rather more specialised type of brake van; this is harbour bank brake No. S55181. The Folkestone Harbour branch was provided with four ex-South Eastern Railway bank brake vans from a very early date and these were replaced by three SR wagons in 1938, Nos. 55180-82. They were constructed on old LBSCR B2X tender underframes, but for some reason the middle axle was taken out – perhaps to maximise the braking effect on four wheels but as the tenders would have had brakes on all six wheels anyway, this seems a retrograde step. The writer came to know the Folkestone Harbour branch in the 1950s, but never recalls seeing one of these vans used – so perhaps they were ineffective as brake vans. They were rarely seen anywhere other than Folkestone or Ashford Works for overhaul, but during World War 2, with Folkestone Harbour almost out of action, they were loaned to the military and used on the nearby Martin Mill Military railway, where rail mounted guns were operating. All three vans were withdrawn in 1969 and they left Folkestone on 24th September in a goods train bound for Acton and thence on to Cardiff for scrapping. *RCR 5589.*

Above: In the 1930s the Southern was anxious to increase the number of vacuum-fitted express freight trains – so would need similarly equipped brake vans. The existing 4-wheeled "pillbox" design rode harshly at speed and the underframe did not lend itself to being vacuum-braked. However, there were 21 LBSCR AC motor luggage vans standing idle at Streatham Hill sidings since the demise of the overhead electric services. A suggestion to convert these into what would have been rather short bogie bolster wagons had not been acted upon, when the idea of converting them to bogie brake vans was hit upon instead. Between July 1933 and January 1934 they were rebuilt, and this was the result – one of the finest goods brake vans to ever run in this country. They were popular with the staff – as they rode marvellously – and were soon nicknamed "gondolas". Here, No. S56262 stands alongside the goods shed and up platform at Dorchester South on 10th July 1956 – indeed, almost any picture of this station taken in the 1935-65 period will show one of these (or the later SR standard bogie van design) standing at this spot. SR Diagram 1580 was allocated to the AC rebuilds and most remained in traffic until the late 1950s – with a few reallocated to the Engineers for a few years afterwards. Although quite a few of the later Diagram 1550 bogie vans survive in preservation, regrettably none of the rebuilds was saved. *RCR 7560.*

Chapter 12

Diesel and Electric Shunters

Above: An example of the successful Maunsell's original trio of shunters dating from 1937. No. 15202 is seen at Hither Green on 10th June 1961, where it had been based since 1956. Built in collaboration with English Electric, they were originally numbered 1, 2 and 3 – this was No. 2 – with the chassis and bodywork completed at Ashford Works and then sent to English Electric at Preston by goods train for the engines and other electrical equipment to be fitted. All three were employed at Norwood Yard where they shunted continuously from 6am on Monday morning until 4am on the following Sunday. Occasionally they did venture out on main line duties, but with a top speed of only 25mph this was found too restrictive. Bulleid produced his own version of the class in 1949, whilst the GWR, LMS and LNER also produced their own versions, again in collaboration with either English Electric, Fowler, Vulcan Foundry or other diesel engine manufacturers. Subsequently this led to the BR 350hp diesel shunter that became known universally as class 08, some 996 of which were built between 1952 and 1962, making this the most numerous locomotive class in the British Isles. The original Maunsell locomotives survived until late 1964, working latterly from Hither Green, Eastleigh and Ashford, withdrawn not because they were worn out, but because so many BR class 08 locomotives were by then available. The original livery was black, later green, finally with black and yellow chevrons. *RCR 15869.*

Opposite: A rather less successful diesel was this unconventional Bulleid 0-6-0 shunter, No. 11001, seen in Ashford Works yard on 25th October 1958. Built at Ashford in February 1949, this was another of the first generation of BR diesel shunters. Equipped with a Paxman 500hp engine it could operate at speeds of up to 36 mph, and was even said to have reached 43 mph in traffic. It had Bulleid's trademark BFB cast wheels of 4ft 6in diameter and was intended as a dual purpose shunter and trip locomotive. Unfortunately it failed on both counts due to gearing issues and was officially withdrawn on 8th August 1959, following a gearbox failure being cut up in the following December, but clearly had not worked for some time prior to this date. Most of its time was spent at Norwood Yard, but it did venture out on goods trains on the main line. Tractive effort was 33,000 lbs – equivalent to a Q1 0-6-0 – so was this another missed opportunity? The original livery was black, later BR green – presumably the livery seen here. *RCR 12936.*

Electric locomotives were, perhaps surprisingly, a rare sight on the Southern. This is the unique Bo-Bo departmental shunter 74S/DS74 – although it may never have carried its identity visibly – at Durnsford Road power station, Wimbledon, on 9th February 1957. Built in 1899 for use on the Waterloo & City line (along with smaller shunter 75s, which stayed there), it was transferred to the power station to shunt coal wagons into and out of the building in 1915, part of which may be seen behind. It remained on this duty until 1965 – looking just as shabby as in the picture – which is how it appeared for most of its life. Some sources say it was painted green, others grey. All agree it just appeared filthy! *RCR 10174.*